the natural world of

BUGS &
INSECTS

the natural world of

BUGS &
INSECTS

KEN & ROD PRESTON-MAFHAM

THUNDER BAY
P·R·E·S·S

Published in the United States by

Thunder Bay Press

An imprint of the Advantage
Publishers Group
5880 Oberlin Drive
San Diego, CA 92121-4794
www.advantagebooksonline.com

Produced by PRC Publishing Ltd
Kiln House, 210 New Kings Road,
London SW6 4NZ

All notations of errors or omissions
should be addressed to Thunder Bay
Press, editorial department, at the
above address. All other correspon-
dence (author inquiries, permissions
and rights) concerning the content of
this book should be addressed to
PRC Publishing Ltd,
Kiln House, 210 New Kings Road,
London SW6 4NZ.

ISBN 1 57145 288 5

Library of Congress Cataloging-in-
Publication Data available upon
request.

Printed and bound in China

1 2 3 4 5 00 01 02 03

ACKNOWLEDGMENTS
The publisher wishes to thank the following photographers and picture libraries for supplying the photography for this book:

© Rod Preston-Mafham/Premaphotos Wildlife for spine image, front cover (top left and top centre) and pages 2, 4, 10 (bottom), 11 (left), 12-13 (main), 17 (inset), 18 (inset), 21 (bottom), 22 (top right), 39 (top), 46 (top), 50 (bottom), 51, 53 (middle left and right, and bottom), 59 (bottom), 67 (bottom), 80-81 (main), 81 (inset, top), 84 (both), 86 (bottom), 87 (bottom), 91 (bottom), 92-93 (main), 95, 98 (top), 100 (top), 103 (top), 110 (bottom right), 116 (left), 120 (top), 121 (top), 132 (middle right), 145 (top left), 148 (bottom), 150, 166-167, 178, 179 (top), 182 (bottom), 183, 184 (bottom), 211 (bottom), 218 (all), 227, 228-229 (both), 231, 232, 237 (both), 238 (top), 240, 241, 242-243 (main), 293 (inset, bottom), 300-301 (main), 302 (top), 309 (bottom), 310-311 (main), 315 (bottom), 334, 336 (inset, left), 338 (bottom), 356, 357 (bottom), 360 (both), 364, 365 (top), 368, 411 (top), 414 (top), 436 (top), 445 (bottom), 479, 484-485 (both), 486, 488, 489 (top), 492 (bottom), 494 (top left and right), 495 and 501;
© Ken Preston-Mafham/Premaphotos Wildlife for front cover (top right, middle left, middle centre, middle right, bottom left, bottom centre and bottom right) and pages 5 (cut out), 6 (cut out), 7, 8 (middle and bottom), 9 (top and bottom), 10 (top left and right), 11 (right), 12 (inset), 14, 15 (bottom), 19 (inset), 20 (all), 21 (top), 22 (top left, middle and bottom), 23 (both), 24-25 (main and inset), 26 (top), 27 (both), 28 (both), 29 (both), 30 (top left), 32 (all), 33, 34 (all), 35, 36 (top left, middle left and right and bottom left and right), 37, 38 (all), 39 (bottom), 40 (both), 41, 42, 43 (all), 44 (all), 45, 46 (bottom), 47 (bottom), 48-49 (main), 50 (top left and right), 52 (bottom), 53 (top), 54 (bottom), 55 (top and bottom), 56 (both), 57 (all), 58 (both), 59 (top), 60, 61 (both), 62 (bottom), 66 (top), 68 (middle and bottom), 69 (both), 71 (both), 72 (top left and right), 73, 74, 75 (bottom), 76 (middle and bot-tom), 77, 78 (all), 79 (both), 81 (inset and bottom right), 82 (inset, top and bottom), 85, 86 (top), 88 (all), 89 (top left and right), 90, 91 (top), 93 (inset, top), 94 (both), 97 (all), 98 (bottom), 99 (both), 101 (both), 103 (bottom), 104, 105 (bottom), 106 (bottom), 108 (bottom left), 109 (both), 110 (top and bottom left), 111, 112 (bottom), 113, 114, 115 (left), 116 (right), 117 (top), 119 (top left and bottom), 120 (bottom), 121 (bottom), 122, 123 (top), 124-125 (all), 126 (all), 127, 128, 129 (bottom), 130-131 (both), 132 (top left and bottom), 133, 134 (top left and right, middle and bottom), 135 (bottom left), 137 (bottom), 138 (both), 142 (all), 143 (both), 144 (both), 145 (middle and bottom), 146 (all), 149 (both), 151 (all), 152 (top right), 153, 154 (both), 155, 156—157 (both), 160 (both), 161 (both), 162 (cut out and bottom), 164 (both), 165 (both), 168 (both), 169 (both), 170-171 (both), 172, 173 (both), 174-175 (all), 176-177 (both), 179 (bottom), 180-181, 182 (top), 184 (top), 185 (both), 186 (all), 187, 188 (all), 189, 190, 191, 192 (cut out and bottom), 193, 194, 195 (all), 196 (both), 197 (both), 198-199, 200, 201 (both), 202 (bottom), 203 (all), 204 (both), 205, 206 (all), 207 (both), 208 (both), 209 (both), 210, 211 (top), 212 (both), 213, 214, 215, 216, 217 (both), 219, 220-221, 222 (both), 223 (both), 224-225 (both), 226, 230 (top), 233 (both), 234-235, 236 (both), 238 (bottom), 239, 243 (inset, top and bottom), 244-245 (both), 246, 247 (both), 248-249 (all), 250 (cut out), 251, 256-257 (both), 258 (all), 259 (both), 260 (all), 261, 262, 263 (all), 264 (both), 265, 266 (both), 267, 268, 269 (both), 270, 271 (both), 272-273, 274-275 (all), 276 (both), 277 (both), 278-279 (all), 280-281, 282 (both), 283 (both), 284-285 (both), 286 (both), 287, 288 (both), 289 (both), 290-291, 292-293 (main), 295 (all), 297 (top and bottom), 300 (left), 303 (all), 304 (all), 305, 306 (bottom), 307, 308, 309 (top), 310 (inset, left), 312 (both), 313 (both), 314, 315 (top), 316-317 (both), 318-319 (all), 320, 321, 322, 323 (all), 324-325 (both), 326 (cut out and bottom), 327, 328 (inset, top and bottom), 328-329 (main), 330 (bottom), 331, 332, 333 (both), 336-337 (main), 338 (top), 340 (both), 341 (bottom), 342 (both), 343 (both), 344 (top), 345, 351 (bottom), 352 (both), 353, 354, 355, 357 (top), 361, 362 (both), 363 (both), 365 (bottom), 369 (both), 370-371 (all), 372-373 (all), 374, 375 (all), 376 (cut out and bottom), 377, 378-379 (all), 380 (both), 381 (both), 382, 383 (both), 384 (both), 385, 386-387, 388 (all), 389, 390, 391 (both), 392-393, 394, 395 (both), 396, 397 (both), 398, 399, 400 (both), 401 (all), 402, 403 (both), 404 (both), 405 (both), 406 (both), 407 (both), 408-409 (all), 410 (all), 411 (bottom), 412, 414 (middle and bottom left and right), 415 (both), 416 (both), 417, 418 (both), 419, 420, 421 (both), 422 (both), 423 (all), 424-425 (all), 426, 427 (both), 428 (both), 429 (both), 430 (both), 431 (both), 432 (both), 433 (both), 434 (all), 435, 436 (bottom), 437 (both), 438, 439 (both), 440 (both), 441 (both), 442-443 (both), 444 (both), 445 (top left and right), 446, 447 (both), 448-449 (all), 450 (both), 451 (both), 452-453 (all), 454 (both), 455 (both), 456 (both), 457 (both), 458-459 (both), 460, 461 (both), 462 (both), 463 (both), 464 (both), 465 (all), 466 (both), 467 (both), 468-469 (all), 470, 471 (both), 472, 473, 474, 475 (all), 476-477 (all), 478 (cut out and bottom), 479, 480 (top), 481, 487 (top), 490 (bottom), 493, 505, 506-507 (main) and 508-509 (all);
© Geoff du Feu/RSPCA Photolibrary for pages 1 (cut out, top), 63 (bottom), 70, 105 (top), 129 (top), 482 (top), 491, 494 (bot-tom right) and 499 (both);
© Jean Preston-Mafham/Premaphotos Wildlife for pages 1 (cut out, bottom), 15 (top), 26 (bottom), 46 (upper and lower middle), 47 (top), 72 (top), 89 (bottom), 93 (inset, bottom), 96, 100 (bottom), 112 (top), 163, 230 (bottom), 296-297 (main), 302 (bot-tom), 306 (top), 358-359, 366-367 (both) and 500;
Richard Matthews/© Wild Images/RSPCA Photolibrary for page 6 (bottom);
© Jonathan Plant/RSPCA Photolibrary for pages 8 (top), 30-31 (main), 62 (top), 63 (top), 87 (top), 108 (top left), 140 (inset, bot-tom), 152 (top left), 253 (bottom), 490 (top) and 492 (top);
© Ross Hoddinott/RSPCA Photolibrary for pages 16 (inset), 148 (top) and 252 (bottom);
© Les Borg/RSPCA Photolibrary for pages 16-17 (main);
© Mark Preston-Mafham/Premaphotos Wildlife for pages 18-19 (main), 36 (top right), 68 (top), 107 (top) and 494 (bottom left);
Philip Sharpe/© Wild Images/RSPCA Photolibrary for page 30 (bottom);
Robert Pratley/© Wild Images/RSPCA Photolibrary for pages 48 (inset), 55 (middle), 329 (bottom right) and 335 (both);
Sue Bennett/© Wild Images/RSPCA Photolibrary for pages 49 (inset), 115 (right), 252 (middle) and 507 (inset, bottom);
George McCarthy/© Wild Images/RSPCA Photolibrary for page 52 (top);
Martin Dohrn/© Wild Images/RSPCA Photolibrary for pages 54 (top), 106 (top), 118 and 119 (top left);
© David Cantrille/RSPCA Photolibrary for pages 64-65, 66 (bottom), 250 (bottom) and 294;
© Duncan I McEwan/RSPCA Photolibrary for pages 67 (top), 107 (bottom), 145 (right), 152 (bottom) and 339;
© Des Cartwright/RSPCA Photolibrary for pages 75 (top) and 140 (inset, top);
© Ron Brown/Premaphotos Wildlife for page 76 (top);
Tim Martin/© Wild Images/RSPCA Photolibrary for pages 82-83 (main) and 502;
Rupert Barrington/© Wild Images/RSPCA Photolibrary for pages 102, 108 (top right), 123 (bottom), 135 (top), 137 (top), 139 (both), 140-141 (main), 341 (top), 348 (bottom), 480 (middle and bottom), 482 (bottom) and back cover image;
© D W Bevan/RSPCA Photolibrary for page 108 (bottom right);
David Breed/© Wild Images/RSPCA Photolibrary for page 117 (bottom);
© E A Janes/RSPCA Photolibrary for pages 132 (top right), 498 (top) and 503;
Papilio/Robert Pickett for pages 135 (bottom right), 136 and 147 (all);
© Phil Bryson/RSPCA Photolibrary for pages 158-159;
Angela Bird/© Wild Images/RSPCA Photolibrary for pages 252 (top) and 348 (inset, top);
John M Gardner/© Wild Images/RSPCA Photolibrary for pages 253 (top) and 351 (top);
© Colin Carver/RSPCA Photolibrary for pages 254-255;
© Stuart Harrop/RSPCA Photolibrary for pages 298-299, 330 (top), 344 (bottom), 348-349 (main), 350 and 487 (bottom);
© Van Greaves/RSPCA Photolibrary for pages 346-347;
© Dorothy Burrows/RSPCA Photolibrary for page 483;
John Downer/© Wild Images/RSPCA Photolibrary for pages 489 (bottom) and 496-497;
© Mark Hamblin/RSPCA Photolibrary for pages 498 (bottom) and 504.

CONTENTS

INTRODUCTION

In this day and age the term 'bug' has a number of completely different meanings. When talking about a bug in relation to health matters we are referring to a bacterial or virus infection. When a professional entomologist is discussing bugs he is referring to one particular group of insects, the order Hemiptera. In this book, however, 'bug' will refer to insects as well as, in the broader sense, to all the other creepy-crawly animals described in it. As well as many of the more familiar insect groups we will also be looking at the millipedes and centipedes, as well as the spiders along with some of their allies, such as scorpions.

No-one has yet produced a verifiably true estimate of the number of species of 'bugs' in existence today but it is probably somewhere between two and three million. Although we have already identified and named hundreds of thousands of these, there are thousands of specimens sitting in museums and laboratories around the world waiting to be named, with probably just as many still waiting to be discovered.

All of the creatures referred to as 'bugs' in this book are in fact arthropods and they have in common a hard outer skeleton—the

Left: There are countless 'bugs' alive on earth at any one time. Here, swarming across Lake Victoria in Africa is a dense cloud of millions of lake flies.

Right: *Haplophilus subterraneus*, one of the soil dwelling centipedes. England.

exoskeleton—and many-jointed limbs. They all have a head and a body divided up into a number of segments, this number varying between the different groups. Their fossil history indicates that the primitive arthropods evolved from soft-bodied worm-like creatures somewhere between 500 and 600 million years ago. These early arthropods lived in water but the land-dwelling ancestors of the insects, the centipedes and millipedes and the spiders appeared some time between 400 and 350 million years ago.

The Centipedes and Millipedes (Myriapoda)

These two groups of animals have a number of similarities and are included in a single scientific group, the Myriapoda. All myriapods have a many-segmented body with a head at the front end. Centipedes, of which in excess of 1,500 species are known world-wide, have a single pair of legs on each segment while the millipedes, with around 8,000 species described, have two pairs of legs on each body segment. They are mainly nocturnal and thus have poorly-developed eyes, capable of distinguishing day and night but not forming clear images.

Centipedes are carnivorous, feeding on other creepy-crawlies. On the head they have biting jaws and behind the head a pair of fangs with which they inject poison into their prey to immobilise it. Most have relatively long legs and are quite fast moving, living under stones, under bark and in leaf litter, and usually coming out at night to hunt. One group are short-legged, long and thin and hunt for their prey beneath the ground in worm burrows.

Top Left: A millipede coiled up defensively. Canada.

Above Left: A serrated millipede, *Lophostreptus sp.*, coiled up defensively on the savanna. Kenya.

Left: *Pararhachistus potosinus*, a warningly coloured polydesmid millipede in a pine forest. Mexico.

Above Right: A warningly coloured giant millipede *Spirostreptus sp.* in the rainforest of Madagascar.

Right: A warningly coloured millipede, *Sigmoria aberrans*, in a Tennessee forest. USA.

Millipedes are much shorter-legged and thus slow moving. They feed on dead and decaying vegetable matter. As a means of defense they produce unpleasant secretions from the body and as a consequence many of them are warningly coloured. The long-bodied cylindrical millipedes can roll up into a coil, while the stouter pill millipedes can roll up in to a ball to protect their delicate undersides from attack. Polydesmid millipedes, on the other hand, have flattened bodies allowing them to slip easily into crevices if attacked.

Top: A *Sphaerotherium sp.* giant pill millipede grazing on rotten wood in
dry forest. Madagascar.

Top Right: A *Sphaerotherium sp.* giant pill millipede rolled up defensively
into a ball. Madagascar.

Above: Turning over a stone reveals a giant centipede *Scolopendra
cingulata*. Spain.

The Insects

At present biologists recognise about 29 distinct groups or orders within the insects. Only about half of these groups contain instantly recognisable species, in large numbers, from most areas of the world and it is these which we will consider here.

All insects have in common a segmented body divided into three distinct regions—a head, a thorax and an abdomen. On the head are the main compound eyes, sometimes some smaller, light-detecting structures called ocelli, as well as the antennae, the jaws and the pedipalps (often shortened to palps). The thorax bears the three pairs of walking legs and, in all but the very primitive insects, two pairs of wings. The abdomen has inside it the main body organs and at the rear end various appendages used during mating. The way in which these basic structures are arranged dictates the group into which any particular insect is placed.

Mayflies (Ephemeroptera)

While all adult mayflies are free-flying during their developmental stages, with the exception of a single species, all live in water. The most obvious characteristics of the mayflies are the way in which they hold their two pairs of membranous wings vertically above the body and the fact that on the end of the abdomen are two or three long, narrow 'tails', (more correctly called caudal appendages). They have biting jaws but they never feed as adults, so these are not used. The forewings are very much larger than the hindwings and males have elongated front legs used for grabbing hold of the females during mating flights. About 2,000 species have been described.

Above Left: A newly emerged adult of the mayfly *Ephemera danica* next to its moulted skin. England.

Above: A mayfly, *Hexagena limbata*, by a lake in South Carolina. USA.

Damselflies and Dragonflies (Odonata)

Around 5,000 species of damselflies and dragonflies have so far been described and they are all predatory, either snatching their prey from the air or from the surface of vegetation etc. As active hunters they have a very mobile head, large eyes, enabling them to pick out moving prey, and well-developed biting jaws. It is relatively easy to distinguish dragonflies from damselflies in flight. Dragonflies are usually larger and more heavily built than damselflies, though interestingly the largest living species of odonate is a damselfly.

Dragonflies are stronger fliers and whereas the two pairs of membranous wings in damselflies are almost identical in size and shape, the base of the hindwings in dragonflies is greater than that of the forewings. At rest, dragonflies sit with both pairs of wings held out horizontally at right angles to the body while most damselflies usually sit with the wings held in contact vertically above the body. The lestid damselflies, however, are just as likely to be seen at rest with the wings held out sideways from the body, much like a dragonfly. The dragonflies are subdivided into a number of groups with common names such as hawkers, chasers and skimmers, relating to their hunting behaviour, while the club-tailed dragonflies have a characteristic club-shaped abdomen.

Right: A male golden-winged skimmer dragonfly (*Libellula auripennis*) at rest in the Okefenokee Swamp. USA.

Below: A male of the large red damselfly (*Pyrrhosoma nymphula*). England.

Far Left: A *Chlorolestes sp.* damselfly by a mountain stream. South Africa.

Left: A male blue-fronted dancer damselfly (*Argia apicalis*) sitting by a pond. USA.

Below: Taking a break from patrolling his territory by a pond is a male southern hawker dragonfly (*Aeshna cyanea*). England.

Main Picture: A male broad-bodied chaser dragonfly (*Libellula depressa*). England.

Inset Left: A female of the four-spotted chaser dragonfly. (*Libellula quadrimaculata*). England.

Inset Below: A female *Libellula pulchella* chaser dragonfly sits on a stick by a small lake in Idaho, USA.

Grasshoppers, Crickets and Katydids (Orthoptera)

All of these insects are contained within the order Orthoptera, which itself is then subdivided into two main groups, one containing the grasshoppers the other the crickets and katydids. (In Great Britain and Ireland katydids are usually called bush-crickets). It is one of the larger orders, with around 20,000 species worldwide. The majority of the orthoptera have well-developed hind legs, used for jumping, large eyes and biting jaws. Both pairs of wings are used for flying but the forewings are leathery while the hindwings are membranous. While the grasshoppers have relatively short antennae, short ovipositors and are active during the day, katydids and crickets have long, thin antennae, long ovipositors and are more active at night.

Many grasshoppers are brightly coloured, jumping long distances or taking flight when disturbed, though some mountain-dwelling species have lost their wings. Monkey hoppers are mainly tropical and closely related to the grasshoppers. Katydids and crickets tend to be more subdued in their colours, many being camouflaged, and they jump rather weakly. Katydids fly well whereas many crickets have a good turn of speed on six legs when danger threatens. A characteristic shared by many orthoptera is the ability of the males to produce sounds to attract the females. One very specialised group is the mole crickets. They do, in fact, resemble tiny moles at first glance, for they have the front pair of legs adapted for digging and live underground feeding on the roots of plants.

Main Picture: The differential grasshopper (*Melanoplus differentialis*) is widespread across the USA.

Inset Top: *Kraussaria dius*, a grasshopper from the Sokoke Forest, Kenya.

Inset Bottom: The true katydid (*Pterophylla camellifolia*), a green leaf-mimic. USA.

Top: A warningly coloured monkey-hopper, *Erucius apicalis*, in the rainforest of Sumatra.

Above: A tropical rainforest leaf-mimicking kaydid, *Cnemidophyllum stridulans*. Peru.

Right: On a tree sits a male cricket, *Phaephilacris spectrum*, with extremely long antennae. Kenya.

Far Right, Above: A warningly coloured katydid, *Poecilogramma striatifemur*, grooms one of his hind legs. Kenya.

Far Right: The characteristic long ovipositor of a female katydid shows up well in this wingless *Saga sp*. Corfu.

Above: A brightly coloured male *Nisitrus sp.* cricket in rainforest. Borneo.

Above Right: A tiny female red-headed bush cricket (*Phyllopalpus pulchellus*). USA.

Right: A pair of mating groundhoppers on a log in the rainforest of Malaysia.

Below: A *Gryllotalpa sp.* mole cricket female. Kenya.

Walkingsticks and Leaf Insects (Phasmatodea)

Although not a very large order in terms of numbers (about 2,500 species described) and not all that easy to find in the wild, they are nevertheless quite well-known on account of their being kept in schools and as pets. Walkingsticks (stick insects in Great Britain and Ireland) usually have a long, thin body and long, spindly legs so that they do indeed resemble sticks. They have long, thin antennae, rather small compound eyes and biting jaws with which they feed on plant leaves. Wings are usually well-developed in the males and often lacking in females. They tend to be nocturnally active, lying around during the day amongst the vegetation on which they feed and looking for all the world like some piece of stick which has fallen down from above and lodged there.

In contrast to the long, thin walkingsticks the leaf insects are short and broad, green individuals resembling a living leaf and brown individuals a dead leaf. Otherwise their way of life is similar to that of the walkingsticks.

Below Left: A mating pair of the large walkingstick *Ctenomorphodes tessulatus* in a eucalypt forest of Australia—the male is the smaller of the two.

Below: A male of the walkingstick *Stratoctes forcipatus* in its typical resting pose on a leaf in forest. Peru.

Right: Not easy to spot, as it is well-camouflaged amongst moss and leaves, is this rainforest *Circia sp.* walkingstick from Madagascar.

Below: An adult *Phyllium sp.* leaf insect in the rainforest of New Guinea.

Earwigs (Dermaptera)

A small order of insects, with roughly 1,200 species, but included here because of their familiarity to us and their interesting life-styles. Their most obvious features are the pair of 'pincers' (cerci) on the end of the abdomen and the very short leathery forewings, which form covers over the carefully folded, membranous hind flying wings. Earwigs are scavengers using their biting jaws to chew up almost anything they find that is edible. Female earwigs are good mothers, keeping their eggs clear of harmful fungi as they develop and then caring for their young for the early days of their lives.

Where does the name earwig come from? Well it was said in days gone by the they liked to crawl into and settle down in peoples' ears as they slept but we now realise that such occurrences are a rare accident.

Below: A sand earwig (*Labidura riparia*), in the desert of Arizona, USA.

Bottom: The rather attractive linear earwig (*Doru lineare*). USA.

Termites (Isoptera)

Although nothing special to look at, the termites are very interesting on account of their life-styles and their architectural and building capabilities. Around 2,300 species have been described, mainly from the tropics, with a few in warm temperate regions. The basic termite has chewing jaws, fairly long antennae and small compound eyes, which may be absent. All known termites in existence today, however, are social and have a caste system including workers, soldiers and reproductive individuals. Soldier termites often have bizarre modifications of the head in relation to their role as defenders of the colony, while the male and female sexual caste are winged to enable them to disperse to mate and found new colonies. While some species of termite just live inside dead and decaying wood others build the often very large and complicated mounds that are scattered around the plains of various parts of Africa. We now know that the above-ground part of the mound acts as a chimney to allow air to circulate and to control the temperature of the mainly subterranean living quarters. All termites feed on plant material of one kind or another. This material is often highly indegestible and they have single-celled organisms and bacteria in the gut to aid digestion. One group of termites builds fungus gardens in their nests and they then feed on the fungi rather than directly on the plant material they collect.

Above: Large headed *Macrotermes sp.* soldier termites guarding workers harvesting dead leaves in rainforest. Malaysia.

Below: The above-ground portion of the nest of the spinifex termite, *Nasutitermes triodiae*, in eucalypt forest. Australia.

Cockroaches (Blattodea)

If it were not for the fact that a number of cockroach species live alongside us and are pests, it is very doubtful that most of us would realise that they even existed, despite around 3,500 species having been described. In the wild most cockroaches live either amongst vegetation or on the ground amongst litter, while a few live a specialised life in caves. They have long, sensitive antennae, fairly large compound eyes and biting jaws with which they scavenge on almost anything that is edible. Just a few feed on highly indigestible wood and, like the termites, have single-celled organisms living in their gut to help break it down. The pronotum covering the top of the thorax is well-developed, the legs are long, for they are usually fast-moving, and the membranous hindwings are covered by the leathery, pigmented forewings. To the uninitiated they resemble beetles, from which they are most easily distinguished by the fact that the forewings of the cockroaches overlap along the centre of the body, while those of the beetles meet exactly. The females are often wingless and the hissing cockroaches do hiss when threatened.

Above: A small cockroach feeding on fruit in Mexican desert.

Below: The large hissing cockroach *Elliptorhina javanica* foraging at night in tropical dry forest. Madagascar.

Above: Eating an assassin bug she has recently caught is a female of the praying mantis *Parasphendale agrionina*. Kenya.

Left: Sitting waiting for prey to alight on the flower in rainforest is a female *Acontista sp*. praying mantis. Trinidad.

Praying mantids (Mantodea)

Along with a few of the katydids the mantids have some of the most bizarre faces to be encountered amongst the bugs, looking as they do like some imagined alien being from a distant galaxy. The main reason for this is that mantids are all eyes, their enormous compound eyes dominating the face and giving them their ability to detect and pounce upon passing prey. 'Praying' of course comes from the way in which they sit with their front arms held up as if they are in prayer. On the underside of their arms are long spines and these help to immobilise a struggling victim as the mantid hugs it before delivering the first, fateful bites. Mantids do not, in fact, have enormous jaws but nibble delicately at their prey, usually demolishing it head first. Most are green or brown in colour, merging into the background, while others mimic sticks or dead leaves. A few are brightly coloured flower mimics. They have a mainly tropical distribution and are a small group with just under 2,000 species known.

Right: The European praying mantis (*Mantis religiosa*), in its typical 'sit-and-wait' hunting pose.

Below: A small *Tithrone sp.* praying mantis female eating a skipper butterfly. Trinidad.

Bottom: A green leaf-mimicking mantis sits atop a twig waiting for passing prey. South America.

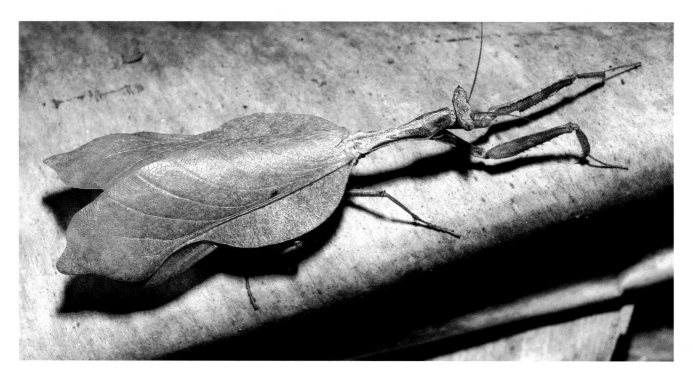

Above: Some praying mantids, such as this male *Acanthops falcataria*, are marvellous dead leaf mimics. Brazil.

Right: A well-camouflaged specimen of the bark-dwelling praying mantis *Humbertiella ceylonica*. India.

Far Right: Making itself appear more formidable than it really is, a nymph of the praying mantis *Polyspilota aeruginosa* in defensive pose. Madagascar.

Below: The 'gin-trap', prey-snatching front legs of a female *Polyspilota aeruginosa*. Uganda.

Bugs (Hemiptera)

In the bugs we have our first encounter with insects that have sucking rather than chewing mouthparts. On the underside of the head, in place of the jaws, bugs have a sucking tube, the proboscis or rostrum, itself evolved from biting jaws, with which they pierce plants or the bodies of other animals to feed. Although all bugs also have compound eyes there are other features on which they are separated into two distinct groups. The plant bugs (the Homoptera) have a rostrum that is held permanently out from beneath the head. In the true bugs (the Heteroptera), however, which include both plant feeders and feeders on other insects and spiders, the rostrum can be tucked back under the body between the legs. Another way to distinguish them is by the way that they hold their wings. Both the plant and the true bugs have two pairs of wings, the hind pair membranous and used for flying, the front pair stiffer, pigmented, often brightly, and used to protect the hind pair. In plant bugs the forewings are held somewhat tent-like above the body and covering the hindwings but in the true bugs the forewings are held flat over the body, with the ends overlapping and the hindwings folded up beneath them.

The true bugs have several families, their common names relating either to their body form or their habits. The shield or stink bugs are broad, flattened insects many of which produce unpleasant odours from special glands to deter attackers. The assassin bugs are aptly named stealthy hunters of other 'bugs', while the leaf-footed bugs get their name from the enlarged and often flattened hind femurs. The mirids are mainly plant feeders and include a number of important pest species. About 25,000 species of true bugs are known, though there are more plant bugs with over 40,000 species described. These include the familiar aphids, the noisy cicadas, the treehoppers, froghoppers and leafhoppers and the bizarre lantern bugs, with their unusual facial extensions.

Right: An adult and nymphs of a *Lyramorpha sp.* shield or stink bug. New Guinea.

Far Right: A *Catacanthus sp.* shield or stink bug in rainforest. Sulawesi.

Above: A couple of adult *Arvelius albopunctatus* shield or stink bugs sit camouflaged on their food plant. Mexico.

Below: Warningly coloured shield or stink bugs, *Agonoscelis rutila.* Australia.

Top: The bizarre horned male of the plataspid bug *Ceratocoris cephalicus* in rainforest. Uganda.

Centre: The curved rostrum beneath the head, which it plunges into its prey, shows up clearly in this *Epidaus latispinus* assassin bug in rainforest. Malaysia.

Above: A rainforest dwelling assassin bug, *Ricolla quadrispinosa*, with a very spiny thorax. Peru.

Top: A *Callidea sp.* warningly coloured shield-backed bug. Gambia.

Centre: A large assassin bug, *Platymeris rhadamanthus,* which produces an offensive odour when intimidated. Kenya.

Above: *Pachylis pharaonis*, a warningly coloured leaf-footed bug on a leaf in rainforest. Peru.

Right: Sitting on a heliconia flower is an adult of the leaf-footed bug *Leptoscelis centralis*. Peru.

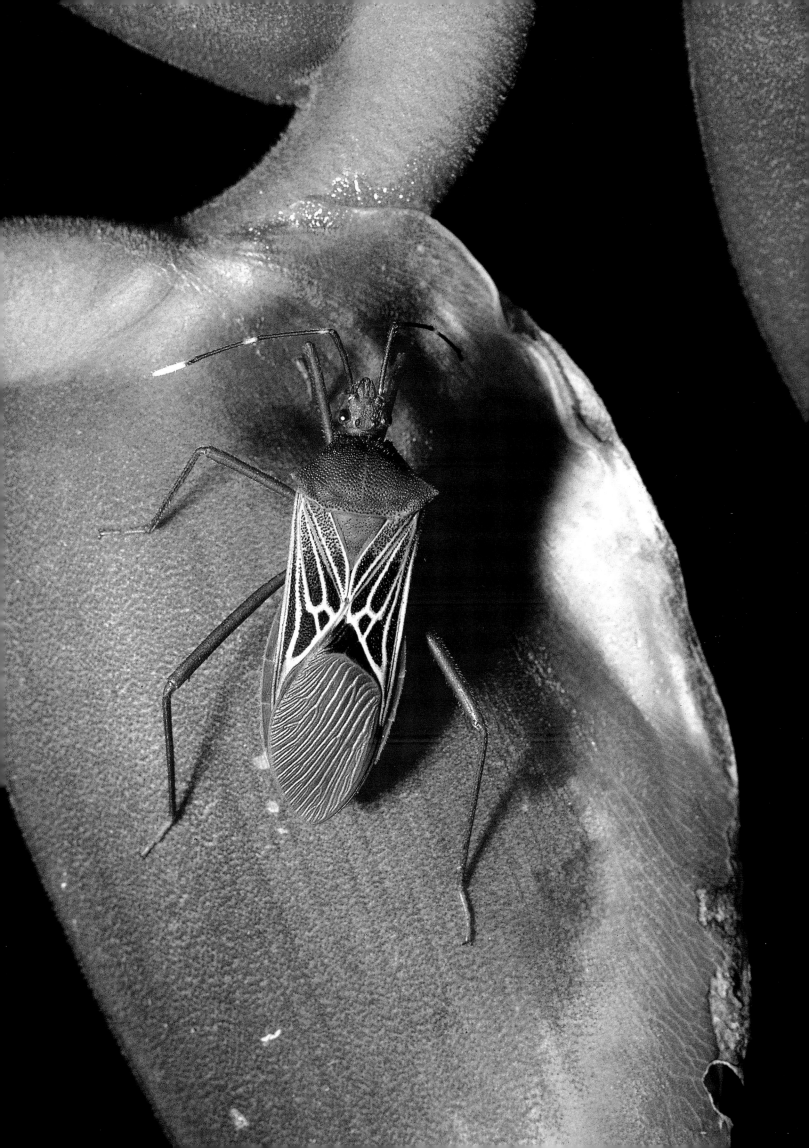

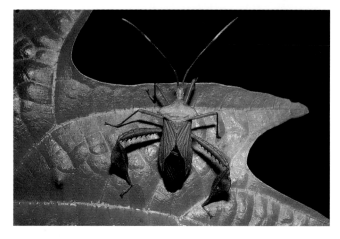

Above Left: An adult *Mictis profana* leaf-footed bug. Australia.

Above: *Paryphyes pontifex*, a very attractive rainforest leaf-footed bug. Peru.

Left: It was possibly new to science when this *Acanthocephala sp.* leaf-footed bug was photographed in rainforest. Peru.

Above Right: Note the flattened segment on each antenna on this *Thasus acutangulus* leaf-footed bug in desert in Arizona. USA.

Right: A male meadow plant bug (*Leptoterna dolobrata*), sits on a grass seedhead. England.

Top: Feeding on a knapweed flowerhead is an adult rosy plant bug (*Calocoris roseomaculatus*). England.

Right: A cicada sits motionless on a tree in rainforest. Borneo.

Above: The broad-headed bug *Mirperus jaculus* on lantana fruits. Kenya.

Top: At rest on a leaf in rainforest is a *Tettigoniella sp.* leafhopper. Kenya.

Above: With its bizarre broadening of the front legs a *Peltocheirus sp.* leafhopper sits on a leaf in rainforest. Peru.

Far Left: A male *Macrotristria sp.* cicada sits on a eucalyptus twig. Australia.

Left: Peculiar body shapes are often found amongst the treehoppers; this is *Sphongophorus guerini* on a vine. Trinidad.

4 3

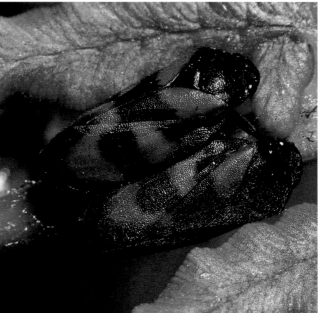

Top: A warningly coloured *Anchistrotus sp.* treehopper in rainforest. Peru.

Above: Mating black-and-red froghoppers (*Cercopis vulnerata*). England.

Left: A lantern bug sits on a tree trunk in rainforest. Sumatra.

Right: The function of its long 'nose' unclear, a *Pyrops sp.* lantern bug sits on a tree in rainforest. Brunei.

Beetles (Coleoptera)

As a group the beetles are perhaps the most successful animals in existence today for more than 300,000 species have been described from around the world. Despite this enormous variety they all have the same basic body structure. Most beetles have well-developed compound eyes and biting jaws. Interestingly, however, a small number have evolved a sucking proboscis with which they probe flowers for nectar. The one feature that separates the beetles from other insects is the arrangement of the wings. The forewings, or elytra, are hardened, pigmented and, when folded shut, meet in a straight line down the centre of the body. At rest the elytra cover the delicate, membranous hindwings which are used for flying.

As you might expect, with so many different species, there are also many different groups of beetles, some well-known, others very obscure. The ground beetles and the tiger beetles, for example, are in the main ground-dwelling predators. Also mainly predatory are the rove beetles, easily recognised by their short elytra, which reach only part of the way down the abdomen. The soldier beetles are not

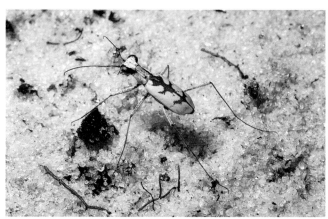

Top Right: The iridescent fiery searcher or caterpillar hunter ground beetle (*Calosoma scrutator*), searching for prey at night. USA.

Above Right: The tiger beetle *Cicindela gratiosa* searches for prey on the sandhills on which it lives. USA.

Right: Tiger beetles, this is *Megacephala carolina*, are often very attractive in appearance. USA.

Below: Showing the typical body form of the family, a rove beetle raises its orange tail as a warning when molested. Trinidad.

Above Right: An eyed click beetle (*Alaus oculatus*), sits on a log in mixed forest. USA.

Right: As it lies on its back the 'peg and socket' click mechanism of the click beetle *Chalcolepidius porcatus* is clearly visible. Trinidad.

palatable to predators and most are brightly coloured while the click beetles are named after the peg and socket mechanism on their underside. This allows them to jump violently and to escape from their enemies when disturbed. The jewel beetles are so-named because a number of them are iridescent blue or green or are very brightly coloured. Probably familiar to most are the ladybird beetles, or ladybugs, which are generally warningly coloured, for they are distasteful, and are important predators of aphids. Also distasteful and warningly coloured are the oil beetles, with many species having larvae which are parasitic on the larvae of mining bees. The scarab family contains the chafers, which are plant feeders, and the dung-rollers, which play such an important part in the rapid dispersal of herbivore dung on the world's grasslands. The stag beetles are well-known on account of the enormous development, in many species, of the mandibles in the male. These are used in fights over possession of the female beetles. The longhorn beetles get their name from the long antennae of many of the family and while the adults feed on oozing sap or pollen the larvae bore into dead or living wood and thus some are pests. The leaf beetles, as their name suggests, feed mainly on plants; they are often brightly coloured. One group are able to withdraw their head and legs and pull the pronotum and elytra tight down on the surface of a leaf when attacked. No wonder that they are referred to as tortoise beetles. The weevils constitute one of the largest beetle families. They all have the front of the face extended to a greater or lesser extent to form a rostrum with the jaws at the tip and in many of them the body is clothed in a dense covering of scales.

Main Picture: The jewel beetle *Stigmodera simulator* feeding on a bottlebrush flower. Australia.

Inset Left: The 22-spot ladybird beetle (*Thea 22-punctata*). England.

Inset Right: A seven-spot ladybird beetle (*Coccinella 7-punctata*), about to take flight. England.

Top Left: A *Mylabris pustulata* oil beetle feeding on a hibiscus flower in rainforest. Sri Lanka.

Top Right: Most dung-roller beetles are black, in contrast to this brightly marked *Helictopleurus quadripunctatus*, which is collecting sifaka lemur dung. Madagascar.

Above: This lovely chafer, the striped green silversmith beetle (*Plusiotis gloriosa*), from Arizona, is becoming rare as a result of over-collection. USA.

Right: The bee beetle (*Trichius fasciatus*), which is feeding on flowers, is a small chafer. Switzerland.

Above: A male European stag beetle (*Lucanus cervus*), with his jaws adapted for fighting.

Right: An orange variegated longhorn beetle (*Tragocephala variegata*), opens its wings for take-off. South Africa.

Top: A six-spotted rufous longhorn beetle, *Protorrhopala sexnotata*, in rainforest. Madagascar.

Above: Perched on its asclepiad food plant is *Tetraopes femoratus*, one of the milkweed longhorn beetles. USA.

Above Right: A tiny warningly coloured leaf beetle, *Lema sexpunctata*, in broad-leaved forest. USA.

Right: *Leptinotarsa juncta*, a leaf beetle closely related to the Colorado beetle, on its horse nettle food plant. USA.

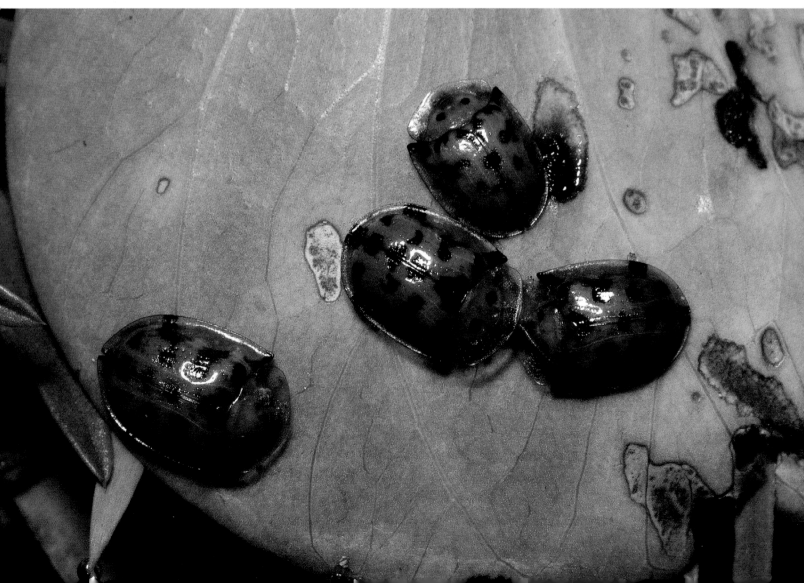

Above: Two male *Aspidomorpha sp.* tortoise beetles pursuing a female across a leaf in rainforest. Sulawesi.

Above Left: A group of brilliant green and blue *Chrysolina sp.* leaf beetles.

Left: A gathering of *Aspidomorpha deusta* tortoise beetles. Australia.

Right: The head of the nut weevil (*Curculio nucum*), showing clearly the hairs which cover the body of many weevils. England.

Below Right: The rainforest dwelling weevil *Belorhynus exclamationis* is found in Malaysia.

Saw-flies, Bees, Wasps and Ants (Hymenoptera)

This is a very large family with more than 120,000 species already described and possibly twice this number actually in existence today. Collectively this group of insects are referred to as the Hymenoptera, which means 'membrane winged'. This is because both pairs of wings are membranous and folded flat over the body at rest. The forewings are always larger than the hindwings and along the leading edge of the hindwings is a row of hooks, which engage with a fold on the hind edge of the forewings to create what is effectively a single large wing. Adults have large compound eyes and biting mouthparts, with the exception of the bees, of course, which have evolved sucking mouthparts. The saw-flies lack the narrow waist of other hymenoptera and their common name comes from the saw-like ovipositor of the female, with which she cuts into plant tissues to lay her eggs.

A number of wasp families, including the ichneumons and the banner wasps, are parasitic in their larval stages, living either inside

Above Left: *Cercidocerus indicator*, a weevil with unusually large antennae. Malaysia.

Left: The weevil *Cholus simillimus* on a leaf in rainforest. Peru.

Top: A female *Tenthredo colon* sawfly laying her eggs into a bracken frond. England.

Centre: Feeding on a hogweed umbel is a warningly coloured *Tenthredo temula* sawfly.

Above: Pupae of a parasite wasp on the body of the caterpillar in which the wasp larvae have been internal parasites. Peru.

Below: A female *Gasteruption assectator* banner wasp searching a cliff face for solitary wasp nests into which she will lay her eggs using her long ovipositor. England.

Bottom: A female ichneumon parasitic wasp sits grooming her back legs on a leaf in forest. Kenya.

Right: Feeding on a flower in desert is a *Scolia sp.* parasitic digger wasp. Mexico.

Below Right: A golden northern bumblebee (*Bombus fervidus*), foraging on a thistle flower. USA.

or on the surface of their 'bug' hosts. The females have ovipositors, which can be extremely long, adapted for locating, penetrating the body of and laying eggs inside the host, often deep inside dead or living wood. The wasps are in the main predators or scavengers. Many are solitary, digging a burrow in the ground or using a ready-made hole in which to lay up provisions in the form of paralysed insects or spiders as a food supply for their larvae. Others make nest cells from mud or live socially in paper nests manufactured from wood scrapings. The bees also vary from solitary to social in their behaviour, again living in burrows or making large nests containing the familiar, waxy, honeycombs. All of the ants are social with, depending on the species, colonies containing a few tens of individuals up to hundreds of thousands.

Left: Workers of *Apis florea*, the small oriental honey bee, on their nest. India.

Top: Weaver ant (*Oecophylla smaragdina*) workers taking prey up a tree trunk to their nest. Malaysia.

Above: The ant *Ectatomma tuberculatum* in typical alert ambush pose on a plant in rainforest. Trinidad.

6 1

Butterflies and Moths (Lepidoptera)

Most readers will instantly recognise a butterfly or moth, so what features do they have in common and how do you tell them apart? In common they have well-developed compound eyes and sucking mouthparts, which may be coiled up at rest. One primitive family of moths has, however, retained biting mouthparts and feeds on pollen. The wings are large and covered in overlapping, pigmented scales resembling feathers, which may also cover the body in some species. In a number of butterflies from different families and in the clearwing moths all or part of the wings have lost these scales, revealing the clear membrane beneath. Separating the moths from the butterflies is more difficult but in general moths fly at night while butterflies fly in the day; moths have broad, often feathery, antennae while those of butterflies are long and slim with usually a distinct club on the tip; at rest moths fold the wings in a tent-like fashion over the body while butterflies hold their wings vertically in contact with one another over the top of the body.

Above: Close-up of a morpho butterfly wing showing the rows of overlapping scales that clothe it.

Right: A citrus swallowtail butterfly (*Papilio demodocus*). Africa.

Below: A swallowtail butterfly, *Eurytides agesilaus autosilaus*, drinking by a river in rainforest. Peru.

Below Right: A common mormon swallowtail butterfly (*Papilio polytes*). Southeast Asia.

Overleaf: The yellow form of the tiger swallowtail butterfly (*Papilio glaucus*) feeding on a garden buddleia. USA.

These differences are in fact totally artificial for there are brightly coloured day-flying moths, which the average person would be unable to distinguish from a butterfly. Similarly, many of the skipper butterflies look more like moths than butterflies and in fact some experts recognise butterflies, moths and skippers as distinct groups. It has become even more complicated in recent years when it has been found that some moth families are more closely related to the butterflies than they are to other moths. Furthermore, the butterflies would appear to be more closely related to the caddis flies than they are to the moths. If, however, we consider that many common moths and butterflies obey the general rules for separating them then for the time being we can maintain them as two distinct groups. Over 150,000 species have so far been described.

In the butterflies we find the whites, which may often be yellow or orange or marked with these colours, the swallowtails, with their long wing extensions, the blues, hairstreaks and coppers and the metalmarks. The largest family is the Nymphalidae, whose members are recognised from the fact that they only have the last two pairs

Top: Well-camouflaged amongst leaves is a green hairstreak butterfly (*Callophrys rubi*). England.

Above: *Emesis mandana*, an example of one of the metalmark butterflies. This example was found in Mexico.

Above Left: Showing just how hairy some butterflies are is a male common blue (*Polyommatus icarus*). England.

Left: A festoon butterfly, a close relation of the apollos, both belonging to the swallowtail family.

of legs fully developed, the front pair being present only as short stumps. In this family are such familiar butterflies as the painted ladies, the peacocks and the admirals as well as the monarchs, the browns and the tropical ithomiines and heliconiines. The skippers are still considered by most entomologists to be butterflies, since they are all active during the day. They also have the clubbed antennae of the butterflies, though their more heavily built body and their wing posture at rest is more moth-like.

The hawk moths and the saturniid moths in particular, contain some of the world's larger species while the arctiids are often highly patterned and warningly coloured. Geometer adults often, though not invariably, have camouflage colouration while their larvae are the familiar 'inchworms' or 'looper caterpillars'. The largest family in the Lepidoptera is that of the noctuid moths, which includes species such as the angle shades and the yellow underwings. In fact the majority of moths that you are likely to encounter fluttering around an outside light during the summer months will be members of this family.

Left: The common European swallowtail (*Papilion machaon*), photographed in Portugal.

Below Left: A metalmark butterfly *Chalodeta theodora* beside a river in rainforest. Peru.

Below: Looking like an enamelled brooch on a leaf in rainforest is the metalmark butterfly *Cremna actoris meleagris*. Peru.

Right: A nymphalid butterfly *Catuna crithea* on the forest floor. Kenya.

Below Right: Drinking from damp ground on the rainforest floor is the nymphalid butterfly *Doxocopa cyane*. Peru.

Left: The monarch butterfly (*Danaus plexippus*), a warningly coloured unpalatable species. USA.

Top: *Acraea caecilia*, a member of a subfamily of nymphalid butterflies that are unpalatable. Kenya.

Above: Some acraea butterflies—this *Acraea quirina* is an example—have partly transparent wings. Kenya.

Top Left: Euptychia hestone is typical of many of the 'browns' in having a pattern of eyespots on the underside of the wings. Trinidad.

Top Right: *Bicyclus dentatus* another of the 'browns' with the typical pattern of eyespots on the underside of the wings. Kenya.

Above: A gulf fritillary (*Agraulis vanillae*), one of the heliconiine butterflies basking on a rock. USA.

Right: In the dark depths of the rainforest an *Oleria sp.* ithomiine butterfly delicately sips nectar from a flower. Peru.

Left: A day-flying, warningly coloured arctiid moth, *Amphicallia pactolicus*, in rainforest. Kenya.

Top: The robin moth (*Hyalophora cecropia*), one of the saturniids. USA.

Above: An *Aethria sp.* clear-winged arctiid moth in rainforest. Peru.

Top: The geometrid peppered moth (*Biston betularia*), showing its camouflage colouration. England.

Above: While many geometrid moths are camouflaged as adults this day-flying *Atyria sp.* is warningly coloured instead. Peru.

Left: *Parachalciope euclidicola*, a warningly coloured noctuid moth, in rainforest. Kenya.

Right: The angle shades moth (*Phlogophora meticulosa*), a noctuid, whose caterpillar eats almost anything and can be a nuisance to the gardener. England.

Flies (Diptera)

Probably the first thing that most people do on seeing a fly is to grab something to swat it with. While a small number of flies are a nuisance to humans and their livestock and crops, by far the majority carry on their lives without interfering with us in any way. All flies lack the more primitive biting mouthparts and have evolved some form or another of sucking jaws. Most are excellent fliers, aided by their large compound eyes and the arrangement of the wings. The flies have only a single pair of membranous flying wings, the forewings. The hindwings are reduced to a pair of roughly club-shaped structures, the halteres, which are believed to act as a form of gyroscope in flight, enabling flies to make the rapid changes in direction so characteristic of them.

Most primitive of the flies are the crane flies and the mosquitoes. Horse flies and deer flies have biting mouthparts adapted for feeding on the blood of vertebrates while the robber flies use their proboscis to pierce the body of insect prey. Bee flies and hover flies may usually be found on flowers, where they feed on nectar or pollen. Conopid flies are usually mimics of wasps or bees and their larvae are parasites of these insects. Dung flies are important for their larvae help to break down the dung of grazing animals, while the adults are predators on other flies.

Top: Most crane flies are fairly drab but *Leptotarsus ducalis gloria* mimics a wasp. Australia.

Above: Although a typical mosquito to look at *Toxorhynchites moctezuma* females feed on nectar rather than blood. Trinidad.

Left: A *Tabanus unilineatus* horse fly, at rest on a tree trunk, has the general appearance of most of its family. Kenya.

Above Right: A robber fly feeds on a flesh fly, which it will have taken in flight. Kenya.

Right: The bee fly *Exoprosopa argentifasciata* feeding on a composite flower. Mexico.

Above: Many species of bee flies, like *Villa cypris* here, have dark patches on the wings. USA.

Main Picture: *Laphria sp.* robber flies are usually mimics of various species of bee. USA.

Inset Below Left: A male common tiger hover fly (*Helophilus pendulus*), on a garden everlasting flower in England.

Below: The common wasp fly (*Conops quadrifasciata*), feeding on a thistle flower. England.

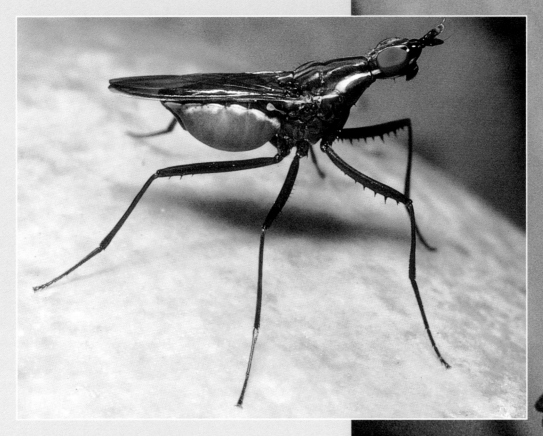

Above: A banana its fly *Nerius nigrofuscus*, sitting on a papaya fruit, has the appearance typical of this family. Trinidad.

Right: A common yellow dung fly (*Scathophaga stercoraria*). England.

Below: Waving its front legs like long antennae and probably mimicking a small ichneumon wasp is a *Mimegralla sp*. micropezid fly. Kenya.

Lacewings and Snakeflies (Neuroptera and Rhaphidopera)

Depending upon the authority, these insects are either all included within the order Neuroptera or else each has its own order. They do, however, have certain features in common and some of them are quite familiar to us. In the Neuroptera are the lacewings, along with which we can include the ant-lions and a rather bizarre group of insects, the mantispids. All have chewing mouthparts and two pairs of roughly equal-sized, membranous wings, which at rest are folded tent-like over the body. The neck region of these insects is somewhat elongated, which separates them from the alderflies and dobsonflies, which have a short neck. At the opposite extreme are the snakeflies, in which the neck is very elongated, allowing them to strike at their prey somewhat in the manner of a snake. Female snakeflies also have a long ovipositor at the tip of the abdomen.

Above: The butterfly-lion (*Libelloides longicornis*), which in flight does look like a butterfly. Spain.

Right: *Palparellus rothschildi*, an adult ant-lion at rest. Kenya.

Below: A giant lace-wing (*Osmylus fulvicephalus*), sitting on a leaf in English woodland.

Arachnids

The arachnids are distinguished from the other 'bugs' in their possession of four pairs of walking legs. Included within this group are the familiar spiders and scorpions, the perhaps less familiar harvestmen and mites and the obscure whip-scorpions and solifuges.

Spiders (Araneidae)

After the insects, which form their main prey, the spiders are the most numerous of the terrestrial arthropods, both in terms of numbers of species and numbers of individuals. All spiders have certain features in common but the group as a whole is divided up into

Above: Exposed by turning over a stone is a male ladybird spider (*Eresus niger*). Italy.

Left: The golden-brown baboon spider (*Pterinochilus junodi*) in savanna. South Africa.

Below Left: Wandering at night in search of a mate is a male desert tarantula (*Aphonopelma iodium*). USA.

Below: A female *Sphodros atlanticus* purse-web spider sitting on the silk of the purse, from which she has been carefully removed for the photographer. USA.

distinct families on the basis of fairly clear differences between them. Unlike the insects, there is no clear separation between the head and the thorax. Instead the head is fused onto the thorax to form a cephalothorax, which is attached to the abdomen by means of a waist. The head region bears biting jaws, the chelicerae, which in all but one spider family are able to inject venom to immobilise the prey. Associated with the jaws are the palps, which the spider uses to test the palatability of potential prey items. Depending upon their family, spiders may have two, six or eight simple eyes, their sizes relating to their lifestyle, web-builders tending to have smaller eyes than active hunters. The thorax region is covered by a tough carapace and it bears the four pairs of legs. With the exception of one very primitive family the spider abdomen shows no clear separations into distinct segments as it does in insects. Apart from this the most obvious feature of the spider abdomen is the occurrence of spinnerets on the tail end, which are concerned with the production of that most important spider product, silk.

The majority of the world's spiders are found in two main groupings. The mygalomorphs are the more primitive and include

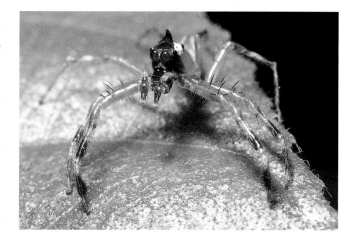

Top Left: Sitting on a leaf in rainforest, feeding on a warningly coloured moth, is a female variable jumping spider, *Eris aurantia*. Mexico.

Above Left: A female leaf jumper (*Lyssomanes viridis*), in tropical dry forest. Costa Rica.

Left: The male of the crested jumper (*Epeus flavobilineatus*) on a leaf in rainforest. Sumatra.

Top, Left: The male two-striped jumper (*Telamonia dimidiata*) is brighter than the female. Sulawesi.

Top, Right: In a stance typical of this family a female *Thomisus sp.* crab spider lies in wait for prey on a flower. Kenya.

Above: A gold-leaf crab spider (*Synaema globosum*) sits waiting to ambush prey in a cistus flower. Spain.

the hairy tarantulas and bird-eating spiders, the trapdoor spiders and the purse-web spiders. Most are medium to large, or very large, spiders with forward-pointing, downward-striking chelicerae.

The rest of the spiders, sometimes referred to as the 'true spiders', are placed into 24 different families. Many spiders are secretive, spending the hours of daylight hidden under stones or beneath bark, while others are active during the day-time and therefore you are quite likely to come across them. The jumping spiders are sun-loving, active hunters, often prettily marked and, though quite small, their large main eyes are visible to the naked eye. The lynx spiders are also large-eyed hunters but do not have the jumping ability of the previous group. The crab spiders, often found sitting waiting for prey to arrive in the centre of flowers, are somewhat flattened and do resemble crabs both in their appearance and in the way that they may scuttle off sideways when disturbed. The giant crab spiders or huntsman spiders tend to have camouflage colours and sit around on bark waiting for passing prey. The wolf spiders are ground dwelling hunters while the fishing spiders and raft spiders are able to run on the surface of water to catch insects which have fallen in or even small fish swimming near the surface.

The comb-footed spiders build a scaffold web and include the notorious widows. The orb weavers are most easily recognised by their vertically spun webs, at the centre of which they like to sit, head down. Although many of them have roughly spherical bodies, a number are very bizarre, with thorn-like or even horn-like extensions of the abdomen. The grass spiders and their large tropical relatives, the golden orb weavers, (their silk is yellow), have much more cylindrical bodies in most species and usually build their webs at more of an angle to the vertical.

Above Right: Carrying her egg-sac speared on her jaws is a female wedding-present spider (*Pisaura mirabilis*). England.

Below Right: The very handsome fishing spider *Dolomedes albineus*, captured on camera in the USA.

Below: *Holconia immanis*, a giant huntsman spider on a tree at night in rainforest. Australia.

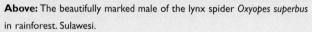

Above: The beautifully marked male of the lynx spider *Oxyopes superbus* in rainforest. Sulawesi.

Left: A six-spotted fishing spider (*Dolomedes triton*), sits waiting for prey on the water at the edge of a small lake. USA.

Below: Outside her burrow is a female *Geolycosa pikei* wolf spider. USA.

Top: Stur's kite spider (*Gasteracantha sturi*), on a leaf at the rainforest margin. Sumatra.

Above: A giant wood spider female (*Nephila maculata*), on her web in the depths of the rainforest. Sumatra.

Right: In her web in the dark depths of a palmetto is a female red-legged widow spider (*Latrodectus bishopi*). USA.

Overleaf: A female black-and-yellow argiope spider (*Argiope aurantia*) in her web. USA.

Harvestmen (Opiliones)

The harvestmen are the one group of 'bugs' that most people are likely to confuse with the spiders. The easiest way to tell a spider from a harvestman, however, is that in the latter there is no clear division at all between the head, the thorax and the abdomen. So if it has eight long legs and no waist then it is a harvestman. They have chelicerae on the underside of the head region but lack poison glands, feeding on small prey or even scavenging on dead creepy-crawlies of one kind or another. On top of the head region is a raised area, the ocularium, which carries the pair of simple eyes. Unlike the spiders, they do not produce silk but run around over the ground and vegetation in search of food. Most have a smooth body but a few tropical species look very bizarre, with thorn-like extensions protruding from the abdomen.

Above: Sitting on a nettle leaf in England is a wandering harvestman (*Mitopus morio*).

Below: Very well-camouflaged stretched along a twig, is the splay-legged harvestman (*Dicranopalpus ramosus*). England.

Bottom: A *Discocyrtus sp.* harvestman, one of the rather bizarre rainforest species. Brazil.

Mites (Acari)

Although the mites never achieve any great size, nevertheless they may often become noticeable on account of their very large numbers. Once again there is no clear division between head, thorax and abdomen but in general they are much shorter-legged than the harvestmen. In mites the chelicerae are modified according to the way in which they feed; those of the parasitic mites being adapted for a piercing and sucking role while those of the free-living mites are used for chewing. The largest mites, and those most often encountered, especially in desert or semi-desert, are the earth or velvet mites, which are covered in a dense layer of hairs.

Tailed whip-scorpions (Uropygi)

Although at first glance easily confusable with the more familiar scorpions, close examination reveals their differences. In this group there is a clear distinction between the cephalothorax and the abdomen, which, unlike that of spiders, is clearly segmented bearing on the end a long, whip-like structure—the flagellum. They have a single pair of small eyes, since they are nocturnal creatures, and the chelicerae do not inject poison. To help subdue prey the palps are greatly enlarged to form grasping pincers. Although they have four pairs of legs, only the rear three pairs are used for walking. The front legs are long and thin and serve a sensory function similar to the antennae of the insects.

Left: Crawling across the North American desert floor is a *Trombidium sp.* velvet mite.

Below: Male and female tailed whip-scorpions courting at night in rainforest. Sulawesi.

Sun-spiders (Solifugae)

Not spiders at all, the sun spiders bear a passing resemblance to the tailed whip-scorpions. Like the latter they use just the last three pairs of legs for locomotion, running at high speed to catch all sorts of small prey, both vertebrate and invertebrate, which they dispatch rapidly with their enormous chelicerae. Both the front legs and the palps are long, antenna-like and used for sensory purposes. The head bears a pair of eyes and the abdomen is clearly segmented but does not have a flagellum. They have a number of alternative common names including wind-scorpions, wind-spiders, sun-scorpions and camel spiders.

Scorpions (Scorpiones)

Whereas the spiders are well-known on account of their wide distribution the scorpions are notorious for their vicious sting. The head bears a pair of eyes on top, providing little in the way of vision

Left: A *Solpuga sp.* sun-spider, face on, showing its huge jaws. South Africa.

Below: A keeled burrowing scorpion (*Opisthophthalmus carinatus*) lurking beneath a stone in desert. South Africa.

since they are mainly nocturnal. On the front of the head the palps are modified as a pair of large pincers, much like those of crabs, and it is with these that most scorpions catch and immobilise their prey before chewing it up with the chelicerae. All four pairs of legs are used for walking. The last half of the abdomen is much longer and narrower than the first half and carries at its tip the stinging capsule. The sting is used to help immobilise larger prey, which the scorpion is unable to subdue with the pincers alone. Scorpions are either burrowers, in which case they normally carry the tail up in the air, or they live beneath stones or bark or in similar places, holding their tails to the side but raising them above the body if threatened.

Above: The scorpion *Buthus occitanus* is usually found beneath stones—its sting is quite dangerous. Spain.

Below: This small scorpion, *Vaejovis carolinensis*, photographed in the USA, lives on the forest floor.

THE MAIN SENSES

Like ourselves, the 'bugs' have a fairly acute set of senses to enable them to go about their everyday lives. The have antennae to feel and smell, eyes to see, ears to hear, palps to taste and an assortment of sensitive body hairs with a variety of functions.

'Bugs' have sense organs and are as much aware of their surroundings as we are and apart from cave-dwellers, which have lost the ability, all of them are able to 'see' to some degree. At the basic level, in those 'bugs' which are either nocturnal or for whom vision is of no use, the eyes are just able to distinguish the difference between night and day or are able to detect a passing shadow. At a higher level we find the compound eyes of insects and the main eyes of spiders, both of which are capable of forming images to a greater or lesser degree. The compound eye can be thought of as containing many single eyes arranged around a curved surface. It is believed that, although such eyes may not form the sharp images that we experience, they are nevertheless better in three dimensions when flying and are also better at picking up small movements, such as that of approaching prey or approaching danger.

Top: The sensitive, comb-like antennae of a male *Rhipicera sp.* beetle in rainforest. Australia.

Above: The huge compound eye of a female southern hawker dragonfly (*Aeshna cyanea*) clearly showing the many facets which make it up. England.

Most spiders have six or eight eyes but only the central pair of main eyes on the front of the face are concerned with image formation. The others are there to detect light and dark and movement. These main eyes are at their highest level of development in the active hunters, especially the jumping spiders. The structure of these eyes is somewhat similar to our own, with a lens at the front of the eye focussing an image onto the sensitive retina at the back of the eye. Here the similarity ends, for in spiders the lens has a fixed focus and it is the retina which moves back and forth to bring about focussing. This process can be seen in action in the larger jumping spiders for you can actually see the eyes flicker as the retina is moved to focus on you as you observe them.

Hearing in 'bugs' is only really of any consequence in those groups, such as the orthoptera and some bugs, which use some form of acoustic communication. At its simplest, hearing involves the ability to pick up any form of airborne vibration, which is all a sound is. Many 'bugs' have no special ear but have, somewhere on the body, sensitive hairs which vibrate in sympathy with the sound

Top: A male *Acrometopa sp.* katydid showing just how long antennae can be in relation to body length in some insects. Corfu.

Above: The face of a large grasshopper, *Krausseria deckeni*, with (between the antennae and just above them) the three simple eyes or ocelli. Kenya.

Left: The large antennae of many male moths—these are of the moon moth (*Actias luna*)—are able to detect just a few molecules of female pheromone. USA.

waves, indicating to them that something, whether it be prey or a predator, is on the move. This type of hearing is normal in the arachnids. Ears with a structure paralleling ours, that is with an eardrum to pick up airborne vibrations, are found, however, in many insects. Despite having the same basic arrangement they are found in different places on the body in different groups, indicating that ears may have evolved independently, several times, in insects. In praying mantids and some moths, for example, the ears are on the thorax, in cicadas, grasshoppers and some moths they are on the abdomen, while in katydids they are on the front pair of legs. Some moths as well as lacewings even have ears on their wings.

Top: The face of a *Chrysops sp.* deer fly clearly showing the hundreds of facets making up the compound eyes. England.

Left: A 'sit-and-wait' predator, the flower mantis *Harpagomantis discolor* has large compound eyes. South Africa.

Right: The fence-post jumper (*Marpissa muscosa*), has large main eyes enabling it to judge the jumping distance to its prey. England.

Feeding

Fossil evidence indicates to us that the earliest insects had jaws with which they broke up solid food of one form or another and the modern equivalent of this system is present in many of today's insect orders. On either side of the mouth of these insects is a pair of tough mandibles, which are used to cut and/or pierce food items and a pair of smaller, finer maxillae, which shred up the food into pieces small enough to swallow. Associated with the mandibles and the maxillae are two pairs of short, mobile appendages, the pedipalps, (often just abbreviated to palps), which are used to feel and taste the food. The mandibles have also taken on other roles for in some beetles they are used to cut holes into wood in which to lay their eggs, while the scoliid wasps use their large mandibles to dig down to the beetle larvae that their own larvae parasitise.

The alternative to feeding on solid food is to feed on some form of liquid and various insect groups have evolved slightly different mechanisms to do this. What is very interesting is that all of these sucking structures are derived in one way or another from the primitive biting mouthparts. Of the insect groups the plant bugs pierce the phloem vessels of plants, from which they obtain a very dilute solution of sugars, amino acids and other substances. Many of the true bugs feed on plants in a similar fashion while others are predators, sucking the body fluids from other 'bugs' or even blood from vertebrates, including humans.

A second major group of suckers are the butterflies and moths but, with a couple of exceptions, they feed on free-flowing fluid such

Above Left: The head of a green tiger beetle (*Cicindela campestris*) showing the sharp jaws with which it transfixes its prey. England.

Left: The head of a large *Acanthophorus sp.* longhorn beetle showing its huge, biting jaws. South Africa.

Above Right: The ground beetle *Scarites terricola* grabbing a darkling beetle as prey in its large, biting jaws. Portugal.

Right: A green tiger beetle (*Cicindela campestris*), feeding on a hover fly. England.

Top: Wasps use their jaws to scrape wood for paper production and to chop up their prey into manageable pieces. England.

Top Right: 'Bugs' with jaws also have to drink and here an ichneumon wasp is taking up water from a leaf. England.

Above: The yellow-faced digger wasp (*Scolia flavifrons*), uses its pointed jaws for digging. France.

Above Right: Larvae and an adult seven-spot ladybird (*Coccinella 7-punctata*) gorge themselves on aphids. England.

Above Right: A leaf-footed bug uses its front legs to groom its very long rostrum. Trinidad.

Right: *Edessa rufomarginata*, a shield or stink bug, with its rostrum piercing a vine stem to feed. Peru.

as nectar, sap, fruit juice or even urine or the liquid on the surface of animal droppings. The exceptions are a few moths which have become blood-suckers. One small group of oil beetles has also taken up the nectar-supping habit and have tubular mouthparts. Most adult hymenoptera feed upon nectar but it is only in the bees that we find a specialised sucking proboscis to obtain it, sawflies, wasps and ants obtaining what they need by effectively 'lapping it up', but much less efficiently than the bees. The final group of suckers are the flies. Some of them, such as the robber flies and the dance flies catch other insects and use their proboscis to pierce the prey and suck out their body fluids. Mosquitoes, biting midges, black flies, horse flies and some others pierce the skin of vertebrates and suck up their blood. Finally, there are those flies which suck up liquid food such as nectar or fruit juices, or pour digestive juices onto solid food and imbibe the resulting liquid.

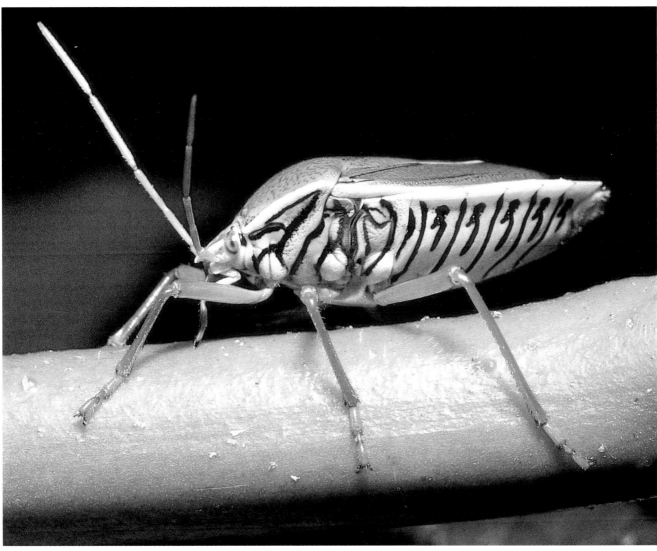

Top: A green-patch swallowtail (*Papilio phorcas*) uses its slim, black proboscis to drink from damp ground. Kenya.

Above: The long, black sucking proboscis of this *Nemognathus sp.* oil beetle can be seen folded back under its body. USA.

Left: Using its proboscis to take nectar from a garden sedum flower is a large white butterfly (*Pieris brassicae*). England.

Right: A *Charaxes sp.* nymphalid butterfly probing dung—the normal food source for this genus of butterflies—with its long proboscis. Kenya.

Foraging and Prey Capture

Foraging is also to do with feeding but involves the actual collecting of food, either for offspring or for the community as a whole in social insects. Perhaps the most obvious foragers are the bees, which collect pollen as a source of proteins and nectar as a source of energy. Bees show a whole range of foraging strategies ranging from being able to collect pollen from almost any type of flower, as in the honey bee and many bumble bees, to being able to use just a single species of flower, as in some of the orchid bees. A few wasps also collect nectar and pollen but the majority of them rely either upon animal food or are scavengers, collecting almost anything that is edible.

Most of the solitary wasps are active hunters, relying upon a particular group of insects or spiders as prey and using their good eyesight and sense of smell to track them down. The prey is then paralysed by stinging and left in the wasp's nest as a source of fresh meat on which the larva can feed. The higher social wasps, however, break up their prey and feed it directly to their larvae. Ants forage in much the same way as the social wasps, though there are specialists, like the leafcutting ants, which collect leaves, grow fungus on them in special gardens and then feed the fungus to the larvae. This is also the lifestyle of some species of those other great social insects, the termites.

Prey capture involves a number of strategies. The hunting wasps, as we have already seen, as well as tiger beetles, many ground beetles and a few ground-dwelling mantids are active hunters, using their large eyes to spot and either run down or pounce on their victims. Most of the predatory bugs either use stealth, to creep slowly up to and impale their victims, or they sit around and wait for their prey to come to them. This latter strategy is used by most praying mantids, which sit motionless until a victim comes within striking distance. Robber flies also employ this 'sit-and-wait'

Above Right: A *Polistes exclamans* paper wasp scrapes honeydew from the surface of a leaf to take back to the nest. USA.

Right: A *Belongaster sp.* social wasp makes her caterpillar prey into a ball to take back to the nest as larval food. Kenya.

method. They usually choose some open vantage point, such as a rock or the end of a twig, moving their head with its large eyes from side to side as they search out flying prey. As soon as they spot something suitable they fly to it, grasp it in the front legs and stab it, usually in the back of the neck, with their tough proboscis. Dance flies employ similar methods but more often amongst vegetation and they have a greater tendency to fly around seeking out their prey.

Prey Capture in Spiders.

Whereas many insects are vegetarians, all spiders are carnivores, feeding mainly upon insects. A few, however, are more specialised and feed upon other spiders or in some instances upon the occasional small vertebrate. The most obvious way in which spiders take prey is the most visible, that is, the web and the one you are most likely to encounter is the orb web, which has evolved in one form or another in at least three families. The web of the garden spider or the argiope spiders is based on a set of non-sticky radii, like the spokes of a wheel, over which is laid a spiral of sticky silk. The whole structure is excellent for catching flying insects. Some spiders insert

a pattern of denser silk, the stabilimentum (see glossary), into the web. It was long thought that this was to show the web up to birds so that they avoided flying through it. More recent investigations have indicated that its function may well be to reflect ultraviolet light, in much the same way as many flowers, and thus to attract insects to it. Sheet webs of one form or another are laid down horizontally and are used in the main to trap jumping insects, which accidentally fall onto them. Above the sheet in some spiders is a series of vertical and horizontal lines, rather like a scaffold, with which insects collide and then fall onto the sheet. Social spiders build interconnecting webs and assist each other in subduing prey, which they then share.

Those spiders that have forsaken the web as a means of prey capture use a different set of strategies. One such is the

'sit-and-wait' method employed by the crab spiders. They sit still on vegetation or flowers waiting for an insect to land close to them. They then grasp them in their strong front two pairs of legs and deliver a fatal bite. The mainly ground-dwelling wolf spiders also 'sit-and-wait', though they are more inclined to move to a new hunting spot if they fail to catch prey at a previous site. The fishing spiders and raft spiders of the genus *Dolomedes* are able to detect vibrations passing through water and can run onto the surface of lakes and ponds to catch small fish or insects that have fallen in. Many of the tarantulas sit either in or at the entrance to their burrows and pounce on insects or other 'bugs' as they walk past.

Rather than sitting and waiting the jumping spiders actively hunt prey, zooming in on it with their large main eyes and jumping onto it from distances up to several times their own body length. Two other strategies are worth a mention here. A number of spiders have become 'lazy' and instead of catching their own prey they enter the webs of other spiders and steal theirs. Perhaps more bizarre are a number of specialists who feed on other spiders. Among these are the rafter spiders, which often build their webs in the corners of rooms in human habitations. These small bodied, long-legged spiders are able to creep stealthily up to and subdue house spiders, which are several times bigger than themselves.

Left: The orb web of the multicoloured orb weaver spider (*Argiope versicolor*). India.

Above: A multicoloured orb weaver spider (*Argiope versicolor*) sits at the centre of the X-shaped stabilimentum in the middle of her web. Sumatra.

Right: A wrapped wasp hanging in the web of a garden spider (*Araneus diadematus*). England.

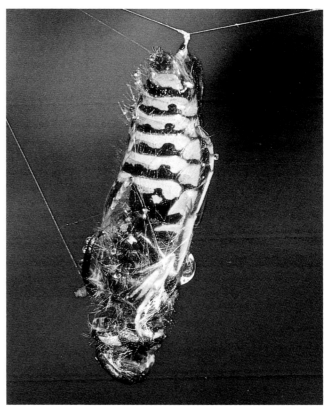

Above: The dew-covered sheet and scaffold web of the dainty platform spider (*Microlinyphia pusilla*). England.

Above Right: A multicoloured orb weaver spider (*Argiope versicolor*) feeds on a cricket that she has caught in her web. Sumatra.

Above Right: Social spiders, *Anelosimus eximius*, in their complex of webs. Brazil.

Right: Webs of a social spider covering an acacia tree in the Masai Mara Reserve. Kenya.

Above: Immature *Dolomedes sp.* fishing spiders often hunt out of water and this one has caught a red damselfly on a waterside reed.

Above Right: A female flower spider (*Misumena vatia*) a 'sit-and-wait' hunter, feeding on a bumble bee. England.

Left: A *Dolomedes sp.* raft spider with a small fish it has caught.

Right: Feeding on a house spider (*Tegenaria duellica*) is a daddy-longlegs or rafter spider (*Pholcus phalangioides*). England.

Courtship and Mating

In order for any form of courting to take place the males and females need to get together. In those 'bugs' that live at very high densities in a particular habitat this may pose no real problems but many live as singles, often widely spaced in relation to their size, and therefore some mechanism is required to get them together. The most common of these is the production of sexual scents or pheromones, which are produced more often but not uniquely by the females. These airborne perfumes allow the males to track down the females, sometimes from distances of several kilometres, as in the case of some moths. As they move around, spiders leave a thin trail of silk behind them and in females this is impregnated with pheromones. Once a male spider picks up the scented silk he is able to follow it to find the female.

An alternative way to attract a mate is to call to it. This strategy is adopted by cicadas and some other bugs as well as by the orthoptera. The sound produced by a large male cicada, when heard close-up, can be almost painful. The amount of energy he puts into calling may be appreciated if you pick a male up and he begins to call for it makes your hand vibrate. The sound is produced by what is

Above: The dark-brown structures at the base of the wings of this male great green bush cricket or katydid (*Tettigonia viridissima*), are used to produce his courtship 'song'. England.

Above Right: A male four-spotted tree cricket (*Oecanthus quadripunctatus*) at night 'singing' to attract a mate. USA.

Below Right: Giant millipedes, *Epibolus pulchripes*, courting, with the male crawling over the female. Kenya.

Below: A newly emerged *Odontotermes sp.* termite queen flaps her wings to disperse pheromones as she 'calls' for a male to mate with. Nepal.

effectively a pair of drums, thin areas of the exoskeleton that are vibrated by muscle action. Sound production in other insects involves rubbing together two parts of the body, referred to as stridulation. Grasshoppers, for example, rub a file on the hindleg against a scraper on the forewing while the katydids and crickets rub the wing-cases together very rapidly. Other methods of sound production include tapping part of the body against the substrate, producing whining sounds by rapid vibration of the wings, characteristic of some flies, and clapping together of the wings in flight, as in some butterflies.

It is hard to grasp the fact that such apparently lowly creatures as the 'bugs' can have complex courtship procedures before mating is attempted. There is no particular pattern within any of the groups with regard to either the simplicity or the complexity of the courtship behaviour in that, for example, some 'bugs' indulge in virtually no courtship whatsoever, whilst others have a long and complicated one. There are far too many different courtships to be able to describe them all, so just a couple of examples will suffice. In many robber flies the males hover behind the females and attempt to stroke them on the back of the head as a prelude to mating. Some of the hover flies employ a similar strategy, hovering above her and then 'bouncing' on her as an inducement to allow mating. Epibolus giant millipede males sit on top of the female and then nibble gently at her face before she allows him to mate with her. In some spiders, courtships can be very brief, the male just walking up to the female and mating with her. In many spiders, however, the male has to convince the female of his intentions by going through some form of courtship. Our thinking is that this is to suppress both the male's and the female's natural predatory instincts, so that they do not mistake one another for prey. Sometimes male spiders do get eaten by their mates and the opposite is sometimes also the case. Garden spider females are often quoted as eating their mates but personal experience of hundreds of meetings between males and females in the wild indicate that if he is careful the male is at little risk when courting the female. Nocturnal spiders tend to have a tactile courtship, the male gently

Below: A desert-dwelling darkling beetle *Lepidochora discoidalis* male chases after a female during courtship. Namibia.

Above: Flying in courtship over a female is a male *Phyciodes actinote* nymphalid butterfly. Mexico.

Left: A male *Euploea sp.* butterfly extracting plant poison with which he will make aphrodisiac chemicals to use during the courtship of a female.

tapping or stroking the female with his legs. The males of large-eyed, free-living species, such as the wolf and jumping spiders, generally use their palps to signal their attentions to the females. Each species has a unique set of signals which prevents accidental mating between species. Web building spiders—the bordered orb weaver is a typical example—have small eyes and vision plays little part in courtship. Instead, the male enters the female's web and plucks at it in a regular pattern to attract her attention. This regularity is unlike the wild strugglings of insect prey and shows the female that it is a male who is approaching. A final interesting strategy employed by some male spiders is to present the female with a gift and then mate while she is feeding. Alternatively he may mate with her just after she has moulted and before her jaws have hardened.

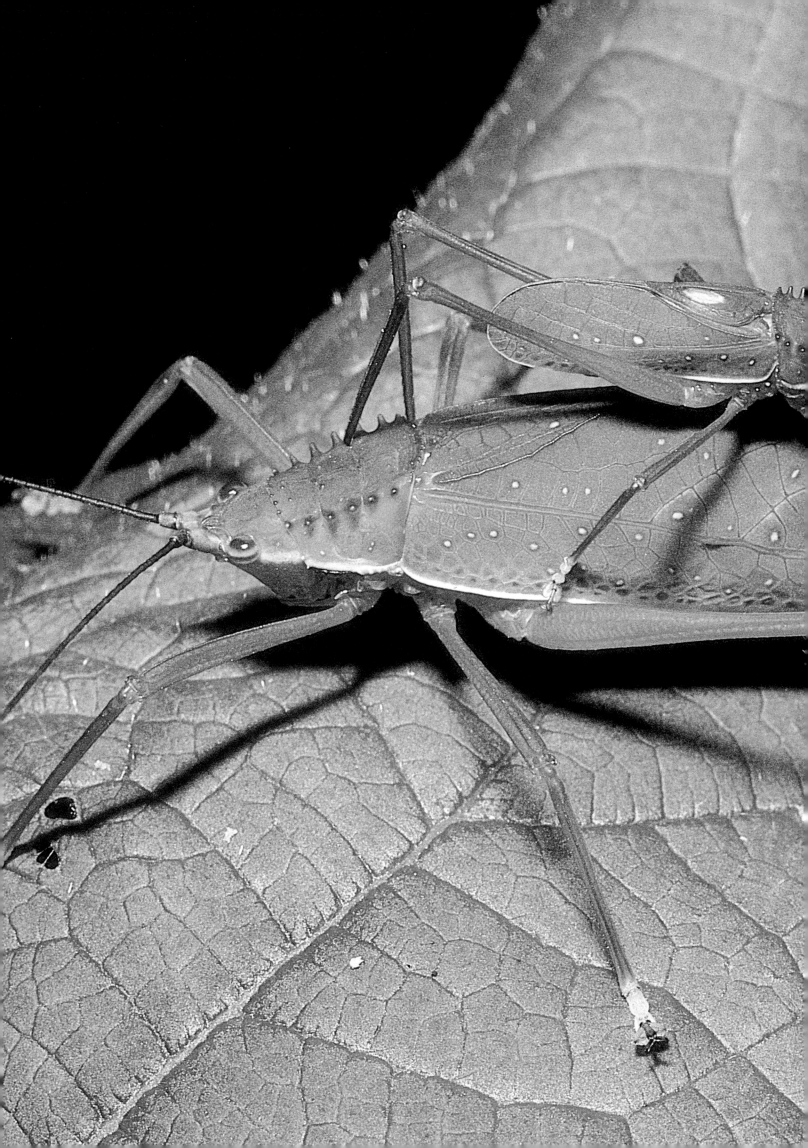

Above: A male *Mallophora sp.* robber fly hovers over a female in courtship. Brazil.

Left: A small male *Chloracantha lampra* katydid courts the larger female in rainforest. Australia.

Below: The smaller, bordered orb weaver spider (*Neoscona adianta*) male courts his larger prospective mate in her web. England.

Mating is an altogether more straightforward process in the majority of 'bugs'. In centipedes there is no direct joining of the male and female. Having courted the female with the same degree of care indulged in by male spiders, for centipedes are also fierce carnivores, the male deposits a drop of semen on a tiny web he has made and the female then runs over it and takes it into her body. This method of non-contact mating is also indulged in by a number of arachnids. In millipedes and the insects the male introduces his penis, or an equivalent structure, into the female and deposits semen directly into her body. Male insects may sit atop the female—grasshoppers are a good example—or may mate tail to tail, as in bugs. Dragonflies and damselflies have a unique mating technique when they adopt the 'wheel position'. The male reproductive opening is at the end of the abdomen and from this he deposits a package of sperm, the spermatophore, into a secondary reproductive area beneath the second abdominal segement. The wheel position is attained when the male grasps the female round the back of the neck, using the end of his abdomen, and she then bends her body under and forwards to engage his secondary sex organs with the tip of her abdomen. In this position she is able to pick up the spermatophore.

Perhaps the most unusual form of mating is that evolved by the spiders. The terminal segment of the palp of male spiders is adapted to introduce semen into the female's reproductive opening. Central to the palpal organ is a bulb and tube, similar to a dropping pipette. The male spider ejects a drop of semen, from his reproductive opening on the abdomen, onto a tiny web that he has specially constructed. He then sucks this drop of semen up into one or both palpal organs. Having successfully courted and subdued the female he then introduces the tip of the palp into her reproductive opening and squeezes the semen into it. It is while backing off, having completed mating, that some male spiders are then attacked and eaten by their mates.

Top: These *Epibolus pulchripes* giant millipedes are mating in the tropical dry forest of Kenya.

Above: A close-up of *Epibolus pulchripes* giant millipedes mating in tropical dry forest to show the male intromittent organ. Kenya.

Right: Mating, in the so-called 'wheel position', are a pair of *Orthetrum sabina* dragonflies. Kenya.

Below: Desert-dwelling grasshoppers, *Phaedrotettix valgus*, mating. Mexico.

Above: A pair of mating green tiger beetles (*Cicindela campestris*), with the male holding the female tightly in his jaws. England.

Far Left: A mating pair of leaf-footed bugs, *Leptoscelis centralis*, on a heliconia flower. Peru.

Left: A male black-striped orchard spider (*Leucauge nigrovittata*) on the right mating with a newly moulted female in her web. Sumatra.

Above: Laying a string of eggs along a grass stem is a female *Thyretes negus* arctiid moth. Kenya.

Right: A male elegant grasshopper (*Zonocerus elegans*) mate-guarding a female who is laying eggs in the damp soil. South Africa.

Life-Cycles

As with all other animals the life-cycle of the 'bugs' begins with the egg. How many eggs are laid and what preparations are necessary before egg-laying varies very much from one group to another and from one species to another but here are a few examples of what is involved. The simplest thing a female can do is to just scatter her eggs in an area where she is able to recognise that there will be food available for her offspring. Stick insects and a number of butterflies adopt this strategy. More carefully, many females choose where to lay their eggs so that the offspring hatch on their food-plant. This is typical of most insects whose offspring are plant feeders. Female bugs and butterflies, for example, have to choose just the right species and sometimes size of plant on which to lay either single or batches of eggs. Yet other female 'bugs' construct a nest or protective cocoon in which their eggs are laid and in some instances they may stand guard over it until the eggs hatch.

In centipedes and millipedes, the arachnids and the orthoptera, earwigs, mantids, termites, cockroaches and bugs the eggs hatch into miniature forms of the adult, though at first the head is large in

Top: A close-up of the 'paper' from which a wasp nest is made. England.

Above Left: A Kenyan *Tarachodula pantherina* female mantis sits guarding her egg-case.

Above: Hairs from a *Stachys lanata* leaf are what this female wool carder bee (*Anthidium manicatum*) is collecting to make her nest-cell. England.

Left: A female *Sceliphron fistularum* mud-dauber wasp inserts a paralysed spider into the nest-cell that she has built from mud. Brazil.

relation to the body, the ratio between them gradually approaching that of adulthood with each moult. The growth phases between each moult are called instars and there are generally five or six of these before the moult to the adult takes place. In all but the insects it may be difficult, apart from size, to distinguish the larger instars from the adults. In insects, however, the instars or nymphs do not have the fully developed wings of the adults. As is often the case in the living world, there are two groups of insects which show some variation from this simple arrangement. Because the developmental stages of the mayflies and the damselflies and dragonflies live under water they have much less of a similarity to the adults, nevertheless they do have the same set of instars as the rest, the final instar emerging from the water to moult eventually into the adult form.

In the remaining insect groups discussed in this book—the beetles, sawflies, bees, wasps and ants, butterflies and moths, flies and the lacewings and their allies—development follows a different path. In this case the egg hatches into a larva, which bears no resemblance to the adult. The larva feeds voraciously, growing rapidly through a series of instars until it eventually moults to form the pupa. Inside the pupa the old larval internal organs are broken down and all of the adult structures gradually develop. Eventually, the fully developed adult emerges from inside the pupal skin.

Below: Inside a cave a female *Heteropoda sp.* huntsman spider carries her silk-covered egg-sac. Sumatra.

Above: Warningly coloured second instar nymphs of the harlequin stink bug (*Tectocoris diophthalmus*). Australia.

Above Left: Standing guard over her batch of eggs is a female harlequin stink bug (*Tectocoris diophthalmus*). Australia.

Left: Warningly coloured third and fourth instar nymphs of the harlequin stink bug (*Tectocoris diophthalmus*), with two in the process of moulting.

Below: Adults of the harlequin stink bug (*Tectocoris diophthalmus*). Australia.

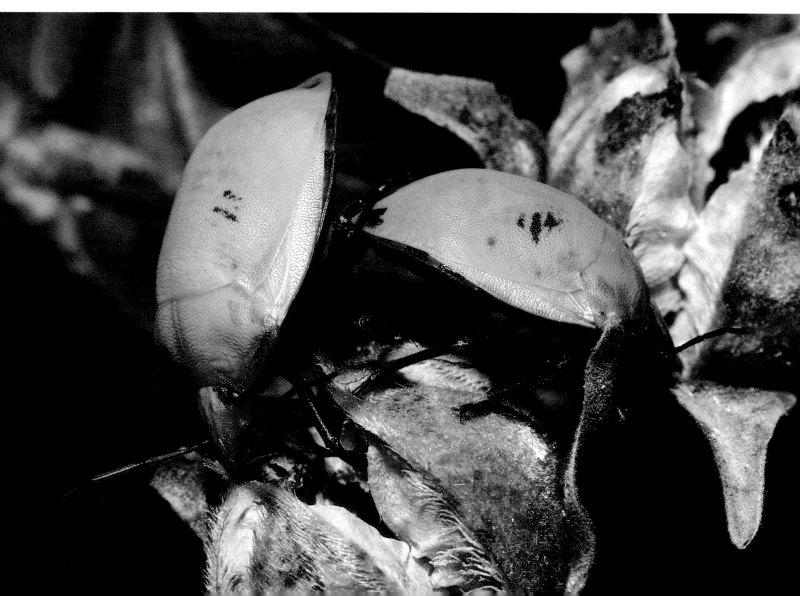

Left: Owl butterfly eggs in close-up.

Below Left: Caterpillar of an owl butterfly. Costa Rica.

Below: An owl butterfly pupa. Costa Rica.

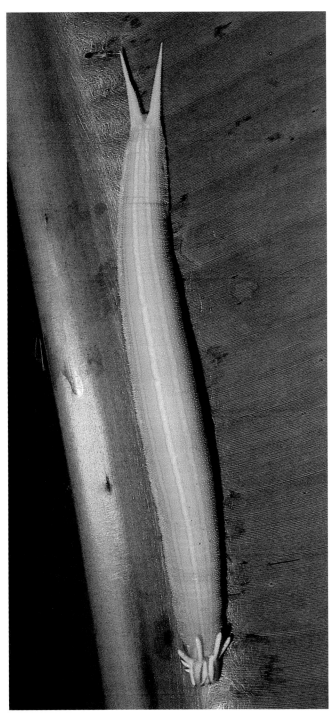

Larvae and Pupae

Insect larvae are pure eating machines, whose function is to process the largest amount of food in the shortest time and grow as quickly as possible. To achieve this end the majority of them have a set of strong jaws with which to demolish their food, which in many species is of plant origin while others are carnivorous. Because most larvae have a relatively thin exoskeleton, allowing them some increase in size between moults, they are quite vulnerable and many have evolved the defense mechanisms described in a later section of this chapter. One extra ploy is for them to gob up the contents of their stomach when they are threatened.

The final larval instar usually chooses some suitable concealed spot in which to pupate and many pupae have camouflage colours. On the other hand, warningly coloured, distasteful larvae may end up as warningly coloured pupae. As a final defense, some larvae weave a silken cocoon, inside which they pupate.

Left: A newly-emerged owl butterfly hangs from the empty pupal case. Costa Rica.

Top: The face of an 'eating machine', the caterpillar of the moth *Eupackardia calleta*. USA.

Above: The warningly coloured caterpillar of the butterfly *Danaus melaneus* feeding on a leaf in rainforest. Malaysia.

Above: The warningly coloured caterpillar of the noctuid moth *Rhanidophora cinctiguttata*. Kenya.

Left: Warningly coloured moth caterpillars. Mexico.

Above Right: The caterpillar of the oleander hawk moth (*Daphnis nerii*).

Right: Caterpillar of the royal oak silk moth (*Antheraea roylei*).

Above: The caterpillar of the robin or cecropia moth (*Hyalophora cecropia*). USA.

Right: The bizarre caterpillar of the hickory horned devil moth (*Citheronia regalis*). USA.

Below: A group of warningly coloured lackey moth (*Malacosoma neustria*) caterpillars on the silk of their protective 'tent'. England.

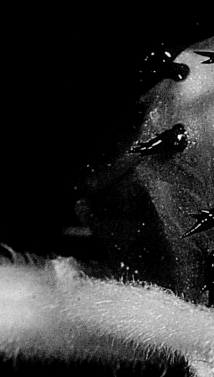

Above Left: The trilobite larva of a *Duliticola sp.* net-winged beetle, which is both armoured and warningly coloured. Borneo.

Far Left: Warningly coloured larvae of the leaden tortoise beetle (*Physonota alutacea*) in tropical dry forest. Costa Rica.

Left: Larvae of the sawfly, *Arge pagana*, raising their tails defensively. England.

Top: The parasitic larva of a pompiliid wasp attaches itself to its spider host. Australia.

Above: A mass of sciarid fly larvae on a wet log in forest. Kenya.

143

Below: A larva of the green lacewing (*Chrysoperla carnea*), feeding on aphids. England.

Bottom: The fierce, predatory larva of an ant-lion in tropical dry forest. Costa Rica.

Right: The warningly coloured pupa of the magpie moth (*Abraxas grossulariata*) in its flimsy silken cocoon. England.

Below Right: The drab colouration of the pupa of the large white butterfly (*Pieris brassicae*) allows it to blend into its background. England.

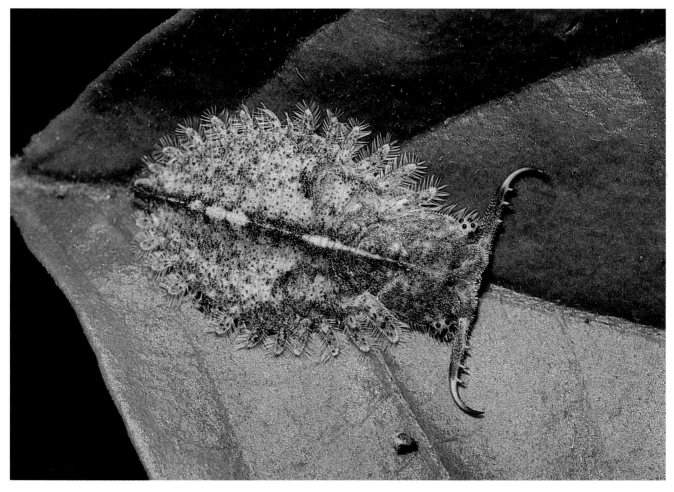

Above: The cocoon of a parasitic wasp hangs from a thread below the corpse of the caterpillar on which the wasp larva fed. England.

Left: The warningly coloured pupa of the glasswing butterfly (*Acraea andromacha*), in wet sclerophyll forest. Australia.

Above: A sequence showing the moulting of the cicada *Venustria superba.* Australia.

Right: Pupa to adult emergence of the peacock butterfly (*Inachis io*). England.

Moulting

In vertebrate animals, like ourselves, growth from baby to adult is a gradual process. In the 'bugs', however, this type of increase in body size is prevented by the fact that the exoskeleton is relatively or totally inflexible. Consequently, in order to grow they have to change the exoskeleton, that is, undergo ecdysis or moult, at regular intervals and replace it with a new one. There is also one group of adult 'bugs' which undergo a regular moult and these are the large, hairy tarantula spiders. The reason for this necessity to moult is quite simple, some of them live for up to 30 years and their outer layers, and the hairs that cover them, wear out and have to be replaced at intervals.

Before the actual moult takes place a new exoskeleton, which is soft and wrinkled, is constructed beneath the old one, with a special fluid separating it from the old exoskeleton covering it. The 'bug' having adopted a suitable position in which to moult, the old exoskeleton then splits from the head back and the animal emerges from it, withdrawing the antennae, legs, and, in insects, the folded up wings, as it does so. What happens next is that it swallows air, which stretches the body, ironing out the wrinkles in the new exoskeleton, with a consequent increase in its size. When present, the folded wings are stretched by pumping blood into the veins which pass through them. Once everything has stretched the new exoskeleton begins to harden and colour. Moulting is very traumatic and quite often fails, resulting in the animal's death. The wings fail to inflate before they harden, for example, or the 'bug' is unable to withdraw its antennae or legs from the old exoskeleton. The latter may still contain a considerable quantity of nutrient material and a number of insects may eat the old exoskeleton after moulting.

Temperature Control

None of the 'bugs' are warm blooded and as a consequence they have to adopt a lifestyle that ensures that they maintain their bodies within a suitable range of temperatures. Looking first at low temperatures, one way of avoiding these is to hibernate and this of course is characteristic of many 'bugs' living in the world's temperate regions. In cool weather activity may be preceded by a period of warming up, either by basking in the rays of the sun or by shivering, which releases heat energy from the muscles.

At the other extreme, of course, they have to avoid excessive heat. A simple way to do this is just to hide from the direct affect of the sun or to burrow beneath the ground. Where this is not possible, another strategy may be used. Dragonflies, for example, have to be around during the heat of the day to hunt prey. Thus they will sit in what is called the obelisk position, with the tip of the abdomen held pointing straight at the sun so that the minimum area of body surface is in contact with its rays. Orb web spiders like to sit at the centre of their webs so that they do not have too far to run to bite and wrap any prey which becomes trapped. Here, they are exposed to the full heat of the sun and a few, therefore, have adopted the strategy of hanging out from the web at an odd angle, thus reducing the area of body exposed to the sun.

Above: A *Polistes fastidiosus* paper wasp sits on her nest and directs a cooling stream of air over it from her rapidly beating wings. Kenya.

Left: A newly-emerged broad-bodied chaser dragonfly (*Libellula depressa*) hangs waiting for its wings to dry and harden before taking its first flight. England.

Below Left: A newly moulted fifth instar nymph of an *Acrometopa sp.* katydid feeds on its old skin. Corfu.

Below: Sitting in the 'obelisk position', with its tail pointing at the sun to reduce heat uptake, is the darter dragonfly *Trithemis arteriosa*. Kenya.

Enemies and Defence

'Bugs' have many enemies. They are the major food source of many birds, insectivorous mammals, lizards and frogs. Their worst enemies, however, are other 'bugs'. What sort of adaptations and strategies can be employed in an attempt to defeat these enemies? Perhaps the most obvious thing to do is to hide, either by diving into a burrow or crevice, or beneath a stone or piece of bark. Alternatively, many insects and spiders have evolved a colouration which matches that of the background—they are camouflaged. Many species take this one step further by both matching the background colour and by mimicking some object, a leaf, a stick, a stone, within the habitat. Both of these strategies demand one important accompanying behaviour; in order to avoid being spotted the 'bug' must sit motionless for much of the time, only moving when necessary, or after dark. Another ploy is to try to startle the enemy, by flashing large eye-spots or patches of bright colours or patterns.

Millipedes and many insects have adopted chemical defenses, which make them offensive or unpalatable, or both. They may either manufacture the chemicals themselves or may make use of nasty-tasting or poisonous substances that they take in from the plants on which they feed. In order to show vertebrate predators that they are not fit to eat, these creatures are often warningly coloured, either being bright red, orange or yellow or having black and white or black and yellow markings. These predators, with their relatively large brains, soon learn to avoid warningly coloured 'bugs'. Other edible species have also evolved warning colouration, mimicking the distasteful ones and therefore fooling the predators.

Right: Warningly coloured *Erechtia sp.* treehoppers being tended by ants. Brazil.

Below Right: A distasteful, warningly coloured *Conderis sp.* net-winged beetle. Malaysia.

Below Far Right: A close-up of the stinging spines of the warningly coloured caterpillar of the saturniid moth *Dirphia molippa*. Trinidad.

Below: The eastern lubber grasshopper (*Romalea microptera*) hisses and produces a repellent chemical foam if threatened. USA.

151

Top: As long as it remains motionless this well-camouflaged willow beauty moth (*Peribatodes rhomboidaria*) is safe from its enemies. England.

Top Right: Mimicking a black ant, which has few enemies, is an early instar of the broad-headed bug (*Alydus calcaratus*). England.

Above: The beautifully marked and camouflaged caterpillar of the Brussels lace moth (*Cleora lichenaria*). England.

Right: The peanut bug (*Laternaria laternaria*)—one at rest with wings closed, the other flashing the eyespots on its wings in a defensive display. Costa Rica.

GIANTS—A SELECTION OF SOME OF THE WORLD'S LARGEST BUGS

Top: A giant cockroach, *Blaberus giganteus*, in a cave full of roosting bats. Trinidad.

Above: One of the world's largest grasshoppers, *Eutropidacris cristata*, can reach 11 centimetres (4.5 inches) in length. Brazil.

Right: The female of the walkingstick *Acrophylla titan* can grow up to 25 centimetres (ten inches) or more in length. Australia.

Above: With the largest wingspan of any lepidopteran, 30 centimetres (12 inches), the noctuid moth *Thysania agrippina* rests during daylight on a tree trunk in Amazonian rainforest. Brazil.

Left: Giant millipedes, such as *Archispirostreptus gigas*, can grow up to 25 centimetres (ten inches) long. Kenya.

Overleaf: Among the world's heaviest moths, is the atlas (*Attacus atlas*).

Above: From the tip of its horn to the end of its abdomen this Hercules beetle (*Dynastes hercules*) measures up to 18 centimetres (seven inches). Costa Rica.

Below: When in flight this giant palm weevil, *Rhynchophorus ferrugineus*, looks like a small bird. Sulawesi.

Above Right: The world's largest known jewel beetle, *Euchroma gigantea*, grows up to nine centimetres (3.5 inches) long. Peru.

Below Right: At rest on a tree in rainforest is the world's largest fly, *Pantophthalmus tabaninus*, which can reach up to five centimetres (two inches) in length.

1 BUGS ON MOUNTAINS

In the British Isles anything over about 500 metres (1,650 feet) qualifies as a mountain. In places such as Peru or Bolivia this would hardly merit the term 'hill' and mountains proper don't begin until about the 1,500 metre (5,000 feet) mark, although the really specialised alpine wildlife is confined to much higher altitudes, above about 3,000 metres (9,850 feet), as on most tropical mountains. Basically, the further away from the tropics you are, the lower the level at which specialised mountain animals will occur.

Mountain 'bugs' are a hardy lot. They need to be, for winters can be cruel, surprise snow storms often spoil springtime days and even summer nights may be frosty. In many mountain systems rain is never far away and summer thunderstorms are frequent. Conversely, huge areas of mountains, such as much of the Andes, the southern Rockies and the Central Asian mountain chains, suffer from varying degrees of aridity. Mountain meadows garlanded with wild flowers might be the norm for the European Alps or the American Rockies but bare rock and scree are more usual in much of the Andes or Scottish highlands, the former the

Left: This *Dolatettix* ground-hopper or pygmy grasshopper mimicks a pebble high on the stony slopes of Mount Kinabalu in Borneo.

Right: The Wasatch mountains, Utah, USA.

Below: A gulley in the French Pyrenees, filled with alpine thistles and irises.

Bottom: The Alps in France.

result of drought, the latter arising from the perpetual diet of cold, damp weather.

The hardiest of the alpine 'bugs' seem to be *Trechus* species wingless ground beetles (Carabidae), which live on the edges of glaciers in the Himalayas at heights of up to 5,500 metres (18,000 feet). One whole group of 'living fossil' insects, the so-called cricket-cockroaches (in the order Grylloblattodea) are almost confined to the most desperately harsh places near the snowline in the Rockies and some other mountains. They live beneath stones and moss and were only discovered as recently as 1914.

Because of the frequent high winds, summer thunderstorms and relatively short growing seasons found on mountains, alpine insects tend to be wingless, especially the beetles and grasshoppers. Many

Right: At more than 4,000 metres (13,000 feet) in the altiplano of the Peruvian Andes a male *Pseudomeloe collegialis* blister beetle dogs the heels of a female through the short, wiry turf. Both sexes are wingless and the orange stripe down the sides serves as a warning of distasteful properties.

Below Right: *Euthystira brachyptera*, a wingless grasshopper from the European mountains.

Previous Page: The wingless grasshopper *Miramella alpina* from Europe.

Below: A *Podisma pedestris* female grasshopper from the Pyrenees in France.

Bottom: This wingless *Parasphena* grasshopper was photographed on Mount Kenya.

Right: *Punacris peruviana* from the high Andes is strikingly similar to *Podisma pedestris* from Europe, yet they are in different subfamilies.

Below Right: *Monistria concinna*, a wingless grasshopper from the Snowy Mountains in Australia. It belongs to the subfamily Pyrgomorphinae, most of which are warningly coloured and distasteful.

Above: *Colias cesonia* at 4,300 metres (14,000 feet) in Bolivia.

Right: The arid landscape of the Argentinian Andes at 3,500 metres (11,500 feet), with a forest of *Oreocereus celsianus* cacti.

of the latter are poor fliers at the best of times, so a gust-ridden mountainside would be a risky place to try taking to the air, making a pair of functional wings pretty well redundant. This makes even more sense when you add to the equation the extra food needed to manufacture the wings, food that could be hard to come by during the brief summer. There are a number of surprisingly similar-looking wingless grasshoppers found on mountains around the world but even though they often look remarkably similar, they are not closely related. Because populations on mountain tops tend to become rather isolated from one another, it may lead to the development of new genetic types, eventually leading to new species, as is already apparently happening in the European *Podisma pedestris*.

In general the Andes of South America are relatively poor in insects, partly because they are often very dry with scant vegetation. The main occupants are a hardy band of upland butterflies, especially various 'whites' and 'sulfers', and a few grasshoppers, such as stick-grasshoppers (Proscopiidae), which lurk unseen among the twiggy plants of the highlands, locally called the 'altiplano'. Two of the

most striking of the Andean grasshoppers are *Meridacris mucujiben-sis* and *Meridacris meridensis* from the spectacular paramo of the Venezuelan Andes. Despite being in the middle of tropics, the paramo's height of over 4,000 metres (13,100 feet) gives rise to a wet, bleak climate with snow-showers at any time of year. Not surprisingly, the dominant plants of the paramo, the 'little friars' (*Espeletia spp*), in the sunflower family, wear overcoats of dense white felt. When thousands of these are packed on a hillside like a crowd of spectactors at a winter football game, the result is one of the most amazing landscapes in the world. Each plant forms a dense rosette, and it is down among their comfortably fuzzy bases that the grasshoppers choose to lead most of their relatively snug lives, basking in the warmth reflected by the silver leaves. Only when the

Left: *Tatochila xanthodice*, one of many Andean 'whites', roosting at dusk at 4,300 metres (14,000 feet) in Bolivia.

Right: *Junonia vestina*, a relative of the familiar North American 'buckeye', is a hardy member of the high Andean butterfly fauna.

Below: A perfectly camouflaged stick grasshopper (Proscopiidae) from the Andean altiplano in Argentina.

Above: *Meridacris mucujibensis* grasshoppers mating on a 'little friar' in Venezuela.

Left and Below: 'Little frairs' dominate the Venezuelan paramo at 4,200 metres (13,800 feet).

Above: An *Arhysosage* male bee trying to mate with a female on a cactus flower in Argentina.

Right: A *Bombus sylvicola* bumble bee queen foraging in springtime in the Colorado Rockies.

sun sneaks a brief look at the scene do the grasshoppers leave their living quarters to feed in the open.

During the transient sunny spells the little friars' yellow flowers are urgently visited by large tawny-coloured bumble bees. As they too have a furry overcoat, bumble bees are particularly well-suited for mountain life, being able to remain active at much lower temperatures than most other bees. In early spring the queens of the lovely *Bombus sylvicola* can be seen foraging busily between occasional snowstorms in the Rockies. As with all bumble bees, the over-wintered queens have to carry out all their early foraging by themselves, building up sufficient stocks of food to produce the first workers. Once these are on hand, although they are rather under-sized, they provide vital assistance in getting the nest into top gear. The males of several alpine bumble bee species are unusual in being strongly territorial, and have enlarged eyes so that from their raised perches they can see both rivals and prospective mates coming. The territory-owner will sometimes put up such a show of force to exclude a rival that actual physical injury may result, something that is ususual in insects—one combatant usually backs off before the going begins to get too tough.

In some of the drier parts of the Andes the commonest bees are species of *Arhysosage,* which restrict their visits to various kinds of cactus flowers, often at altitudes above 4,000 metres (13,100 feet) so these are true alpine bees. The small females often don't even wait for the flowers to open fully, but eagerly force their way in when the petals are only just starting to part. Cactus flowers are very rich in both pollen and nectar, and are available even in a dry year when other plants might miss flowering altogether, so they comprise a reliable and bountiful source of food for bees. Because the females only visit cactus flowers, the males know where to find them, and lie in wait on a comfortable bed of pollen, waiting for the guaranteed arrival of a female. These hard-working little bees make really effective pollinators, and the cactus flowers set abundant fruit.

Courtship activity is something else that is triggered by the welcome warmth of the sun. *Cyrtopogon* robber flies are typical of mountainsides in Europe and North America, and the first glimpse of the sun peeping out from behind a slow-moving cloud is the trigger for a vigourous display of courtship. In Europe the red-horned robber fly (*Cyrtopogon ruficornis*) can usually be found sitting around in pairs on a stone or bleached log, the male facing the female a short distance away. When the sun breaks through, the male launches into his fashion parade as he bobs and dances in front of the female, showing off his glossily black-tipped abdomen with its ruff of golden hairs. *Cyrtopogon auratus* from the Rockies is similar and also has an elegant cavorting and bobbing courtship dance, but in both species the male's efforts earn scant reward, and mating success is appallingly low.

Courtship finesse is absent from the repertoire of the brown arctic (*Oeneis chryxus*). This butterfly is common in the arctic tundra of much of Canada, but further south it is restricted to mountains. The males form spaced-out groups, known as leks, on patches of bare ground, and simply wait for a female to fly in. It is she who chooses which of the waiting males will be her mate. This very well-camouflaged butterfly seldom flies so is not often noticed, but the most typical of mountain butterflies, the 50 or so different kinds of Apollos, will be far more prominent. Although they are members of the swallowtail family, these splendid butterflies lack tails, and have strange semi-transparent wings frosted with a thin rime of white, attached to very fat, hairy and noticeably leathery bodies. Apollos are found in the mountains of North America, Europe and Asia, and

Below: A courtship 'dance' by the male red-horned robber fly *Cyrtopogon ruficornis* on the left. France.

are true alpine creatures, absent from the warmer lowlands. Both the caterpillars and the adults are poisonous when eaten by vertebrate animals such as birds, which usually back off after an exploratory bite at the tough leathery body. However, some mammals, such as chipmunks, are not so fussy, and will chew away until nothing is left. This is surprising, as the body fluids have an irritant effect on human skin. Adult Apollos have a rather laid-back fluttering kind of flight that seems to acknowledge the lack of airborne enemies, at least until chipmunks learn to fly! There is no courtship, the males simply go on lengthy patrols for females. After mating, the male tries to ensure that he alone will fertilise his mate's eggs by gluing-up her genital opening, forming a kind of bespoke chastity belt called a sphragis. This is quite large in Apollos, and protrudes prominently from the tip of the female's abdomen, giving advance notice to any pursuing males that they might as well look elsewhere.

One particular genus of 'browns', *Erebia*, has proliferated throughout the mountains of Europe, Asia and North America, with dozens of closely related species, often each restricted to a single small area. Like most 'browns' they are not particularly colourful, and spend much of their time basking on the ground with their

Above: A brown arctic butterfly (*Oeneis chryxus*). USA.

Below: The water ringlet (*Erebia pronoe*) in the French Pyrenees.

Overleaf: Apollo butterfly (*Parnassius apollo*) in the French Pyrenees.

Above: Crown fritillary (*Speyeria coronis*) in the Rockies.

Above Left: Pearly checkerspot (*Chlosyne gabbii*) in the Rockies on an April day.

Left: The Rocky Mountain skipper (*Polites draco*).

wings open. Such basking is especially important in mountain butterflies, which can only become active when there is sufficient warmth, and this is often available only in a narrow zone near the ground.

Many common butterflies breed in warm lowland regions and then migrate up into the highland meadows for their summer feast of flowers, much as European pastoralists still drive their flocks up into the alpine meadows for their summer bounty. The lovely crown fritillary (*Speyeria coronis*) on the West Coast of the USA completes its larval development in the warm, dry lowlands, but then as an adult heads up onto the flowery mountain slopes, returning again in autumn to lay eggs in the lowlands. Many other common butterflies

exist as separate races or subspecies in the mountains, such as the American pearly checkerspot (*Chlosyne gabbii*). Sometimes it can be difficult to decide just where one species ends and another begins, so that the Rocky Mountain skipper (*Polites draco*) may just be a mountain race of the much commoner saltgrass skipper (*Polites sabuleti*).

Biting flies can be a real problem on mountains and tiny black simuliids can make life a misery near sparkling mountain streams in which the larvae breed. In the American Rockies *Symphoromyia* biting snipe flies (Rhagionidae) can be persistent and painful visitors to bare human arms and hands. This is a highly unusual member of its family, most of which do not appear to feed as adults, so the blood-letting habits of this mountain denizen are particularly interesting. A much larger and more striking bristly fly, whose taste in living meat arises at an earlier stage, is the handsome *Adejeania vexatrix*, which is often common in the Rockies in late summer, bustling around on flowers such as ragweeds and thistles. Its larva develops as a parasite within the bodies of various large moth

Above: The Andean hover fly *Copestylum parina* on a llareta flower.

Below: *Adejeania vexatris* in mountain forest in Arizona.

caterpillars, a gruesome habit which is common within its large family, the Tachinidae. In some tachinid species the female lays an egg directly on the caterpillar, but others strew eggs around on the caterpillar's food plant where they are likely to be eaten by accident. Once inside the caterpillar, the egg hatches and the fly larva begins its grim task of consuming the unfortunate caterpillar from the inside out.

One of the highest flies in the world is the rather sombre-coloured hoverfly *Copestylum parina* from the Andes, where it lives on the altiplano at over 4,000 metres (13,100 feet), just below the upper limit of vegetation. Here the ground is white with frost every morning, but by midday the tough little hover fly is busily feeding on its favourite food, the tiny but numerous flowers of the weird llareta plant. This member of the carrot family forms rock-like resinous green mounds like solidified green foam, and is one of the hardiest plants in the world.

THE WEIRD MOUNTAIN GRASSHOPPER

Despite its common name, the mountain grasshopper (*Acripeza reticulata*) is not a true grasshopper, but belongs to the katydid family, Tettigoniidae. Nor is it restricted to mountains, although it is most common in Australia's Snowy Mountain ranges, the highest in the land. When at rest, either on the ground or pressed against the trunk of a eucalyptus tree, the mountain grasshopper looks like a lump of dark bark. If disturbed, such as when prodded by a beak or finger, it bows its head and raises its dark wing-cases, revealing that the top of its shiny abdomen is startlingly banded in blue, red and black. This is a classic warning display, a 'keep off at your peril' notice that the possessor of the bright colours would make a pretty unpleasant mouthful.

Top and Above: The 'before and after' warning display of the mountain grasshopper (*Acripeza reticulata*) from Australia.

Africa's Drakensberg Mountains

The Drakensberg mountains run down the eastern spine of South Africa, and although not high by African standards, they are far enough south to have many mountain species that are not found in the lowlands. These mountains are particularly rich in chafer beetles, many of which are covered with a dense pelt of protective hairs, such as the woolly-bear chafer (*Diathermus tomentosus*). The two-spotted chafer (*Popillia bipunctata*) often forms balls of males on mountain flowers, all heaped up around a single female and struggling to be first to mate with her. In common with other species of *Popillia*, the female plays very, very hard to get, and leads all the eager males on for many days until she finally submits to the lucky winner.

Several spectacular grasshoppers are resident in the Drakensberg, including *Dictyophorus spumans*. If threatened, this large beast raises its rather stubby wing-cases to lay bare its banded black, yellow and red abdomen in all its shiny and very garish splendour. Just to emphasise the 'keep off' message, the grasshopper will also often splay upwards its red and black back legs. Like many of these large and colourful African grasshoppers, it smells absolutely terrible when handled, yet despite this, and all the

Top: Scaly flower beetles (*Anisonyx lepidotus*) in the Drakensberg mountains.

Above: Two-spotted flower chafer (*Popillia bipunctata*) eating a flower. South Africa.

Right and Below: The South African Drakensberg mountains in summer.

Above: *Dictyophorus spumans* forma *olivaceus* grasshopper in full defensive display.

Right: A woolly bear chafer (*Diathermus tomentosus*). South Africa.

Below Right: The mountain beauty butterfly (*Aeropetes tulbaghia*).

warning displays, some individuals still get their wing-cases torn to shreds by birds taking an over-prolonged exploratory peck. The grasshopper itself indulges in a highly unpleasant diet, which includes the spiny leaves of aloes, something few other animals will touch because of the acrid sap.

Most of the butterflies in these mountains are 'browns' and so therefore pretty dull, but one stands out from the rest; the mountain beauty (*Aeropetes tulbaghia*), which is often found feeding on the tubular flowers of red-hot pokers.

A NEW MOUNTAIN MOTH

Although the Andes can be rather unproductive for the bug-hunter, they do hold some pleasant surprises. The author discovered this beautiful moth perched during the day in full view on the white-woolly top of an old man of the Andes cactus (*Oreocereus trollii*) in Bolivia at an altitude of some 4,000 metres (13,100 feet). Not only is the moth a species quite new to science, but it is also probably represents a new genus as well. As relatively little collecting of 'bugs' takes place in the Bolivian Andes, it is probable that there are other such fascinating discoveries still to be made.

Above: A new Andean moth discovered by the author.

MOTH EQUIVALENTS

The transparent burnet (*Zygaena purpuralis*) is the commonest and most widespread of the burnet moths, family Zygaenidae, found on European mountains. Its Andean equivalent is *Cyanotricha bellona*, of the family Dioptidae. Both moths feed actively on flowers during the day-time and are slow-moving and warningly coloured. The transparent burnet is particularly toxic as, like all burnets, it contains a substantial dose of highly poisonous hydrogen cyanide.

Above: Transparent burnet (*Zygaena purpuralis*) in the French Alps.

Right: *Cyanotricha bellona* moth in the Peruvian Andes.

2 BUGS IN DESERTS

There is no such thing as a 'standard' desert. Nor is there any agreement upon what constitutes a desert, although a prolonged absence of rainfall and high summer temperatures are probably the two most widely accepted defining qualities of deserts. Even within this definition deserts vary enormously, from the large areas of totally barren moonscape found over much of the Atacama-Sechura desert of Chile and Peru, to the incredibly plant- and animal-rich hillsides of the Sonoran desert in Mexico and the southwestern USA. One thing is certain: many deserts are very far from being deserted, especially after summer rains, when an exciting menagerie of life is on offer, most of which will be 'bugs' of one kind or another.

Left: A gold-spangled jewel beetle (*Julodis humeralis*) appears after rains in the Kalahari.

Right: A giant millipede coiled defensively in the Kalahari.

The Deserts of Southern Africa

Southern Africa has a diverse array of deserts, including the Kalahari, Namaqualand and the strange and unique Namib. The Kalahari is a paradise for the big-game enthusiast, but the 'bugs' are neither abundant nor distinctive, although there is an abundance of huge black millipedes, which wend their way across the red sands, and a number of brilliantly coloured jewel beetles (Buprestidae) breed in the acacia trees that dot the landscape and are home to the attractive tree rat.

Namaqualand encompasses the northwestern part of Cape Province. In spring there may be a brilliant carpet of wildflowers, accompanied by a permanent display of succulent plants, many of which mimic pebbles.

Much of the Namaqualand desert consists of multicoloured outcrops of shiny crystalline quartzite rocks, interspersed with broad swathes of shimmering white quartz pebbles and broad expanses of reddish sandy soils. With rock and sand outgunning green plants for most of the year, survival for many of the local 'bugs' means looking as much like a piece of rock as possible. Several kinds of *Lamarckiana* toad grasshoppers precisely mimic the streaky patterns of the quartzite rocks. The incredible *Trachypetrella anderssonii* goes one step further, and actually looks so much like a lump of quartz that you could put it down anywhere and just take it for a stone. It is faithful to its local background—white when on shining quartz, ebony when on black outcrops only a short distance away. Natural selection at its most obvious.

Some of the local beetles don't just look like rocks, they are almost as hard as them as well, such as the large *Brachycerus tauriculus*. Like most weevils, when molested it tucks its legs in and dives onto the ground, where it shams dead and looks like a pebble. One particular *Hyboproctus* darkling beetle has even stranger habits, sitting hunched down in full view on lichen-speckled rocks, relying on its knobbly exterior to blend in with the surroundings. Another group of darkling beetles, such as *Somatichus* and *Eurychora* are much more mobile, and spend much of the day trotting around in the burning sun looking for food or a mate. As protection both from the sun and the prying eyes of enemies, they cover their backs with a sprinkling of the local soil.

The *Psammodes* darkling beetles or 'tok-toks' use rocks in a different way. They gain their common name from the male's habit of

Top: The spectacular *Trachypetrella anderssonii* is the best of the stone-mimicking toad grasshoppers from Namaqualand.

Above, Left and Right: The weevil *Brachycerus tauriculus* in normal and 'shamming dead' modes.

Left: *Lamarckiana* grasshoppers perfectly mimic the streaky quartzite in Namaqualand.

knocking the tip of his horny abdomen against a rock, producing a rapid and very penetrating 'tok, tok, tok, tok', sound, designed to attract a mate from afar in this barren landscape.

Although large vegetation is sparse in Namaqualand there is a sprinkling of small trees, especially acacias, home to the zebra katydid (*Terpnistria zebrata*). Acacia leaves are arranged in a ladder-like pattern of light and dark, into which the zebra katydid's pattern of white stripes on a dark green background blends perfectly. When the trees die or become aged they shed twigs and small branches onto the ground, and these are mimicked by stick mantises. The acacias also provide breeding sites for longhorn beetles, such as the strikingly marked *Zographus oculator*, which may appear in some numbers after rains. These may also signal the appearance of hordes of brown-veined white butterflies (*Belenois aurota*). This is a famous migrant, which follows the rains as they develop through the southern African deserts. The fluttering crowds of migrants have an uncanny knack of arriving just when there is a new flush of rain-induced plant-growth, perfect fodder for caterpillars.

The Namib is a long narrow strip of land down the southwest coast of Africa. Despite being the driest of the African deserts, the

Top: *Eurychora* beetle with sand-covered back.

Above: *Psammodes* 'tok-tok' beetle.

Above Right: The stripes on the zebra katydid (*Terpnistria zebrata*) blend in well with the acacias on which it lives.

Right: Migrating brown-veined whites (*Belenois aurota*) drinking on damp ground in the Kalahari desert.

Overleaf: A stick mantis in Namaqualand.

reddish sands and silvery white quartzite plains of the Namib are cloaked in dense dripping fogs for about two-thirds of the year. These fogs derive from the pesence of the cold Benguela current close onshore, which also leads to cool nights. There is virtually no permanent vegetation, except along the courses of the dried-out rivers. Yet bugs are found almost throughout the Namib, so what do they eat? The answer lies far away inland, where the climate is less arid. Winds blow a continuous supply of detritus, such as dead leaves, seawards into the Namib, and it is this supply of material that is the basis of life for many of the Namib's 'bugs'.

The most prominent insects in the Namib, by an overwhelming amount, are darkling beetles, of which more than 200 different species occur, mostly not found elsewhere. Their zig-zag tracks across the smooth faces of the dunes resemble a miniature railway gone mad. Look in any direction, and you will see little shiny black forms plodding or scurrying across the sand. Some 'hot-rod' species have long stilt-like legs, which keep the body well away from

Top: Darkling beetles cluster round a dead grasshopper in the Namib desert.

Above: A typical Namib desert landscape.

Left: *Zographus oculator* longhorn beetle from Namaqualand.

Above: *Someticus bohemani* is one of the more strikingly coloured of the Namib's many darkling beetles. Unlike most of the others, it lives on exposed rock outcrops.

Left: *Lepidochora discoidalis* darkling beetle male plodding relentlessly after a female.

Above Right (Right and Left): One of the smaller Namib darkling beetles, *Stips dohri*, doing its disappearing act into the sand.

Right: *Cauricara eburnea* is one of several long-legged white darkling beetles which live on the quartz plains of the Namib.

the hot sand. They always seem to be in pairs, or even trios, which poses the question, why? The answer is that most of the Namib darkling beetle females are very aloof towards their males. In *Onymacris rugatipennis*, the males spend about one-fifth of each day trailing along in the wake of females. The idea is to stay as close as possible until nightfall, when the female will bury herself in the sand for the night, and mate with any nearby male. Trying to be that nearby male is a real problem: there are so many competitors with the same idea that wrestling matches often break out over who 'owns' a particular female. The males of some other species have an even harder time—their females will sometimes mate, but only on a whim. All the males can do is doggedly follow along all day long in the hope that something will happen. The poor males dare not even

stop to eat when the females pause for a snack, in case a rival barges in, so they have to go hungry.

Most of these legions of beetles never stop to drink. When the sun gets too hot, they stay cool by going to ground beneath the sand, where the temperature can be less than half what it is on the surface. Even though dried leaves might not seem very promising as a source of moisture, their digestion does in fact release quite a lot of water, amounting to nearly half the original weight of the material. Some of the Namib beetles have gone one step further and cash in on the abundant fogs by constructing special channels in the sand on the crest of the dunes. By sitting head-down in these, with their backs pointed seawards, the incoming fog condenses on the beetles' bodies and trickles down towards their mouthparts.

Some of the Namib's darkling beetles are covered with a kind of waxy coating that cuts down water-loss and filters out the strongest of the sun's rays. The inhabitants of the dazzling white quartz plains are themselves often white, which reflects the worst of the heat, and they have long spindly legs to keep them in the slightly cooler air above the roasting quartz.

The other most commonly seen 'bug' on the dunes is the large white hairy ant *Camponotus detritus*. Life is so hard in the Namib that, unlike most ants, their nests contain no stores of food. The ants constantly quarter the dunes for anything that is vaguely edible, including seeds, dead insects and even bird and lizard droppings. They also tap the sweet honeydew secreted by several kinds of scale insects which live on some of the tough grasses that grow on the dunes. After dark, *Comicus* crickets emerge from their burrows to feed. They have sand-shoe feet, broad and rather hairy, designed for sure-footed walking on shifting sands. The shallow burrow of the white lady spider incorporates sand grains into its silken roof, which collapses into the waiting arms of the spider when a cricket walks over it.

In a few places the barren sands of the Namib are spotted with the broad, pale green, shred-ended leaves of the strange upside-down plant (*Welwitschia mirabilis*). The plump female cones of this ancient survivor are often covered with colourful throngs of the

bug *Probergrothius sexpunctatus*. Like most of their family (Pyrrhocoridae) the bugs are warningly coloured in all their stages, and the three dark black stink-gland openings can clearly be seen on the backs of the orange nymphs.

Above: Both adults and nymphs of these *Probergrothius sexpuncatus* bugs on *Welwitschia mirabilis* are warningly coloured.

Below: When workers from different nests of the ant *Camponotus detritus* meet during foraging trips they will kill each other if they can.

New World Deserts— the Atacama-Sechura

Like the Namib, the Atacama-Sechura of Chile and Peru is a long narrow strip coastal desert which enjoys little or no rain but has life-saving quantities of fog rolling in off another cold offshore current, the Humboldt, which also keeps temperatures within reasonable limits. Many parts of the Atacama-Sechura are the driest areas on earth and have never had rain while some areas have a fascinating endemic flora which includes many cacti. Every few years there is a so-called 'el Niño' event, with drenching rains that turn the lifeless desert into a sea of mud, soon followed by brilliant carpets of wildflowers germinating rapidly from long-dormant seeds.

In dry years (that is, most of the time) there are relatively few 'bugs' on view. Some pass the lean times as eggs or pupae, others, such as the bees, sleep the drought away in a state of suspended animation below ground. When the rains come, the vegetation, which appears almost overnight, can be richly decorated with thousands of garish hawkmoth caterpillars, not seen for 20 years or more, while bees fuss busily on the abundant flowers. However, the resiliant cacti provide flowers every year, providing a harvest for a few bees and flies that appear on an annnual basis. Some of the striking *Copiapoa* cacti also provide involuntary sustenance for a jewel beetle, *Ectinogonia buqueti,* whose larvae bore holes through the soft succulent centres of plants, which ooze an evil-looking black liquid from the damaged areas.

Darkling beetles are much less in evidence than in the Namib, whose detritus-based survival-system is absent. The scant vegetation is usually just sufficient to sustain a few black and white *Gyriosomus luczoti,* whose wind-blown skeletons sometimes occur in thousands around the base of a cactus. Several species of *Pseudomeloe* blister beetles also nibble on what little vegetation there is, often in gullies where salt-tolerant plants are present throughout the year in saline flushes.

Left: Thousands of *Copiapa cinerea columna-alba* cacti in the Atacama desert.

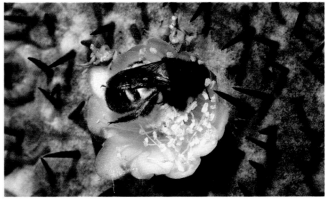

Above: Leafcutter bees make good pollinators of the *Copiapoa* cacti. Chile.

Left: Because of its long legs, the hover fly *Copestylum concinnum* is less effective at pollinating *Copiapoa* cactus flowers. Chile.

Right: *Gyriosomus luczoti* is one of the more boldly marked of the Atacama's many species of darkling beetles. Chile.

Below Right: A *Pseudomeloe* blister beetle in the Atacama desert of Chile.

Below: This *Ectonogonia buqueti* jewel beetle will have spent its larval life burrowing inside this *Copiapoa cinerea* cactus. Chile.

Other New World Deserts

In the New World, deserts occur as far south as southern Patagonia and as far north as British Columbia. Within this area there are several distinct desert types, varying in altitude, topography, vegetation, temperature and aridity. In the north, the hottest, driest and least biologically rich desert is the Mojave of western Arizona and adjacent California and Nevada. To the east and south of this lies the much richer Chihuahuan desert, a vast wilderness of mountains and basins stretching from Texas and New Mexico far down into central Mexico. Sandwiched between and Mojave and Chihuahuan deserts is the Sonoran, possibly the best of them all, extending from southern Arizona way down into Mexico. This is a visually stunning desert, with forests of giant cacti and abundant wildlife.

The South American deserts are much less diverse and interesting. Many lie above 2,000 metres (6,500 feet) in the Andes, so come under mountains rather than deserts. This leaves a relatively small area in Argentina known as the Monte, which florisically has a number of things in common with its northern counterparts, although it is much poorer in 'bugs'.

Above and Below: The Sonoran desert in April shows the high density of perennial plants in this species-rich region. Because of a dry winter, there are few annuals in flower.

BUGS AND CACTI

Cacti are often the most prominent feature in some New World deserts. Unlike annuals, which only appear and bloom after plentiful rains, cacti are always there, and flower reliably every year. Several kinds of leaf-footed bugs (for example, *Narnia*, *Stalifera* and *Chelinidia*) only live and feed on cacti. In the Andes, the strange hump-backed black weevil *Huarucus* cacti inhabits the dense hairy stems of *Espostoa* cacti. Some cactus flowers are long-lived, and in hedgehog cacti (*Echinocereus*) last for many days. They are favourite ambush-sites for bee-assassin bugs (*Apiomerus spp*), which patiently squat on the carpet of pollen, waiting to pounce on an unwary bee. Some bees only visit cactus flowers. *Lithurge echinocacti*, for example, is particularly drawn to barrel cacti, whose generous supplies of

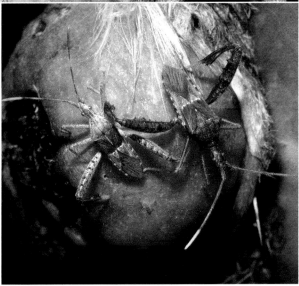

Top: The bug *Chelinidia tabulata* (Coreidae) lives only on cacti.

Above: *Narnia inornata* bugs (Coreidae) on a *Pilosocereus* cactus fruit in Mexico.

pollen allow the little females to collect a full load from just a single flower. The males lie in wait on the flowers and make a nuisance of themselves trying to mate with the overworked females.

Large, over-ripe cactus fruits are eagerly visited by many butterflies, and more especially by ants, for which they may be a vital source of moisture. The ants tear open the fruits, sup on the sweet liquid and extract the seeds, carrying them away to their nests. They drop a few by accident, thereby dispersing the seeds, and in some South American cacti it can be difficult to find a ripe fruit which has not been plundered of all its seeds by the ants. Such efficiency is not surprising, as many ants, such as *Camponotus* carpenter ants, secrete a volatile pheromone that brings new recruits hurrying to help with the work. Carpenter ants derive their name from a habit of nesting in trees and root systems, although some nest in soil.

The large columnar 'cardon' cacti are favourite nesting sites for wasps, who seem to value the additional defence given by the spines. When the paper nest of a *Polistes* wasp is attached to a cactus, it is easy to see that the narrow black stalk which connects the

Above: *Narnia* bugs (Coreidae) mating on a prickly pear cactus fruit in Arizona.

Above Right: A cactus flowers is a perfect ambush-site for this *Apiomerus* bee-assassin bug, sitting beside the discarded body of an *Agapostemon* bee in New Mexico.

Right: The flame-orange blooms of a *Ferocactus wislizenii* barrel cactus flower are the arena for a fight between male *Lithurge echinocacti* bees. USA.

nest to the plant is covered with a shiny black substance. This is derived from the wasps' abdominal secretions, and is reinforced by regular bouts of smearing. Its main purpose is to protect the static, and therefore highly vulnerable nest from invasion by ants, which find the black substance highly repellent. In *Polistes* the queen maintains her dominance over her workers either by eating any eggs they lay or by regular bouts of bullying, the exact method depending on the species involved. The nest may be founded by a single queen, who is later joined by her own offspring, or by helpers from a different nest, who co-operate to support the dominant queen.

Above: Giant cacti are popular nest-sites for paper wasps. This is *Mischocyttarus immarginatus* on their small nest in Mexico.

Above Left: A prickly pear cactus fruit is plundered by *Aphaenogaster* ants in the Chihuahuan desert.

Left: *Camponotus* carpenter ants raiding a prickly pear cactus fruit in Mexico.

Overleaf: This newly-established nest of the paper wasp *Polistes instabilis* on a prickly pear cactus shows the shiny black nest-stalk very clearly. Mexico.

Desert Jewels

A characteristic feature of the Sonoran and Chihuahuan deserts is the high proportion of warningly coloured 'bugs', which feed on the wide variety of poisonous and noxious-smelling chemically-protected plants found in this region. The 'protection' for the plants is often in theory only, as many insects soon learn to cope with the chemical armoury and redeploy it in their own defensive interests, coupled to warning colours. Members of the milkweed family (Asclepiadaceae) and potato family (Solanaceae) are both common in these deserts, and are left well alone by all except their own spe-cial 'bugs'. Milkweeds always seem to be host to a dozens of brilliant red or orange beetles and bugs which can cope in various ways with the acrid latex contained in the leaves and stems. Monarch butter-fly caterpillars (*Danaus plexippus*) often cut off the latex supply to the leaf they want to eat by biting a channel in its stalk, causing it to sag and form a choke-point. The huge sombre-coloured adults of various *Pachylis* bugs (Coreidae) defend themselves actively by turn-ing their rear-ends towards the enemy's face and squirting it with a powerful jet of noxious liquid. The nymphs form spectacular warn-ingly coloured groups on the shoots and twigs of various plants.

Dactylotum painted and rainbow grasshoppers are gaudy creatures which in late summer are often found in hundreds sitting boldly around on the ground or on low plants. Having no need of escaping hurriedly from enemies, they are wingless and move slowly and clumsily around on the ground. The beautiful red and yellow *Perixerus laevis* from southern Mexico is also wingless, as are many of the larger lubber grasshoppers, which rely on expelling a revolting froth when molested, often accompanied by the sudden flashing of brilliant red 'keep away' wings where these are present. The *Neobarrettia* katydids pack a ferocious bite, and when molested respond by flicking open their boldly spotted wings, holding the pose for several seconds until the threat subsides.

Velvet ants (Mutillidae) have a truly ferocious sting, which is advertised by the frequently bright uniform worn by the often very densely hairy females as they scurry tirelessly around on the desert floor looking for the nests of bees or wasps in which to lay their eggs. Most mutillids develop as parasites on the food supplies

Below: The male *Sagotylus confluentus* (left) has much thicker back legs than the female; they are probably used in wrestling-matches with rival males. Mexico.

collected by their hosts and intended for their developing offspring. The intensity of their sting has earned the name of 'cow-killers' for some of the larger North American species, such as *Dasymutilla klugii*. The stingless males are much larger than the females, who are swept off their feet and into the air as part of the normal mating tactic in these insects.

Top: *Dactylotum* painted grasshopper in Mexico.

Above: Upon being touched, the *Neobarrettia vannifera* male flashes his brightly patterned hindwings. Mexico.

Left: The nymphs of *Sagotylus confluentus*, a coreid bug, form warningly coloured groups. Mexico.

Above: On the salt flats of Utah a female *Pseudomethoca propinqua* velvet ant is exploring the nest-entrance of her *Ammophila aberti* sand wasp host.

Left and Below Left: The ornate checked beetle (*Trichodes ornatus bonnevillensis*) occurs in two distinct colour forms. USA.

Right: A spectacular group of Pachylis bug nymphs in Mexico.

Overleaf: When at rest on vegetation, this male *Neobarrettia vannifera* katydid is quite difficult to see. Mexico.

Most checkered beetles (Cleridae) are warningly coloured, and several species are quite common in the western deserts. They are usually found on flowers, where they eat pollen and other small insects, such as thrips. Clerids generally have interesting larval habits, and are often known as 'bee wolves'. In many species the eggs are laid on flowers, where the larvae attach themselves to bees or wasps and hitch a ride to their nests, where they make a meal of the resident larvae.

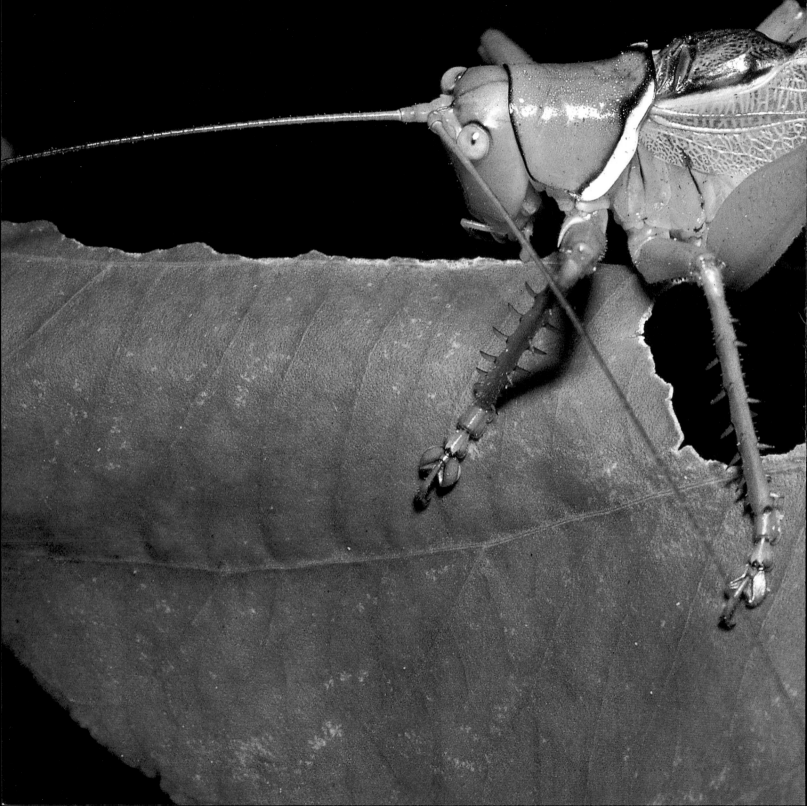

DESERT CAMOUFLAGE

Whereas unpalatable insects advertise this fact with their bright colours, tasty ones need to keep a low profile. As in the African deserts several species of New World grasshoppers are good stone-mimics, notably the toad lubber grasshoppers (*Phrynotettix*), squat little pebble-like creatures that remain invisible until they move. Many other grasshoppers simply blend into lichen-covered rocks, or match the colour of the desert floor, such as the cream grasshopper (*Cibolacris parviceps*). This spends the day resting discreetly on the ground, climbing at night up into the creosote bushes (*Larrea tridentata*) that are their sole source of food. The creosote bush grasshopper proper (*Bootettix argentatus*) spends the day-time on the bushes, where its colouration blends perfectly into the dull green leaves.

One of the most unlikely dwellers on the hot desert floor is the noctuid moth *Forsebia perlaeta*, whose colouration blends well into the rocks and stones on which it spends the day. Another even stranger noctuid *Schinia masoni* passes the daylight hours on open

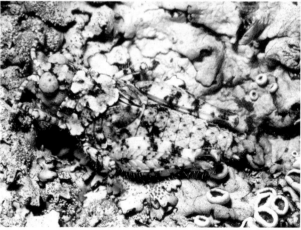

Top: A creosote bush grasshopper (*Bootettix argentatus*) on its food plant in Mexico.

Above: Springtime in the Sonoran desert and a grasshopper nymph is perfectly camouflaged against a lichen-covered rock as it basks in the sun.

Above Right: The cream grasshopper (*Cibolacris parviceps*) blends well into the desert floor. USA.

Right: Looking like a chip of limestone rock, this *Phrynotettix* toad lubber grasshopper in the Sonoran desert is impossible to spot until it moves.

view on the flowerheads of red and yellow daisies. The moths usually arrange themselves so that their yellow foreparts are over the row of yellow outer florets, while their reddish wings are over the red centres.

In the deserts of central Mexico, the leaf-footed bug *Mozena lunata* lives on mimosas. These have ladder-like leaves, similar to the African acacias, and the backs of the *Mozena* nymphs are striped in a camouflage strategy similar to the African zebra katydid—same problem, same solution. The adult bugs are not striped, but neither are they so restricted to their food plant, and they can fly away when threatened.

Above: The noctuid moth *Forsebia perlaeta* spends the day roosting on the desert floor. USA.

Left: *Schinia masoni* moths in their characteristic resting pose on a desert flower in Arizona.

Overleaf: The stripes on this *Mozena lunata* bug nymph (Coreidae) help it blend in with its mimosa food plant. Mexico.

Desert Carnivores

Spiders are not usually very conspicuous in the New World deserts. The larger orb-weavers are relatively rare, probably because the summer is too hot for them on their exposed webs. Most desert spiders live near the ground and many, such as the *Aphonopelma* desert tarantulas, live beneath it. They solve the heat problem by living deep inside cool burrows during the day, emerging at night to prowl the rapidly cooling desert floor in search of food. On certain summer nights hundreds of males may be on the move, bitten by the urge to go in search of the far less adventurous females inside their burrows. During mating, the male holds the female's fangs open with special spurs on his front legs. These large spiders feed on insects, lizards and other small animals, but are relatively harmless to man, with a bite no worse than a wasp's sting. Many other smaller spiders of various families spend their whole lives under stones or bits of wood. The velvety black female of the Arizona black hole spider (*Kukulcania arizonica*) stands guard over her egg-sac inside a silken tube which retreats beneath a stone or a crevice in a wall. A number of silken lines, consisting of no fewer than four kinds of silk, radiate from the mouth of the tube, forming a web designed to catch crawling prey.

Placed just above the ground, the broad sheet-webs of the desert grass spider (*Agelenopsis aperta*) are common in many desert areas. When the summer heat in some of the more extreme habitats, such as open rocky lava-flows, becomes too much to bear, the spiders move out to neighbouring grassy areas, where the heat is less intense. The broad sheet web is designed to trip up and catch hopping insects such as grasshoppers, although the spider itself can run across the treacherous tripline-laden sheet with ease.

Below: Arizona hole spider (*Kukulcania arizonica*) guarding her egg-sac.

Above: Desert grass spider (*Agelenopsis aperta*) at the mouth of its silken tube. USA.

Right: The female of the western desert tarantula (*Aphonopelma chalcodes*) is a formidable creature. USA.

The jumping spiders (Salticidae) are often active despite the summer heat. The males are often brilliantly coloured with an orange or crimson uniform, contrasting with the dull females. The males use their eye-catching attire in complicated courtship dances which employ their legs and palps to best effect in a series of attractive and complex moves. Jumping spiders are efficient killers, able to catch insects much larger than themselves, such as grasshoppers and even small dragonflies.

After summer rains huge numbers of vivid scarlet velvet mites may be seen milling around on the desert floor. The adults feed mainly on insects' eggs, and so may be important in controlling their

numbers. The immature stages of the mites are usually attached to the legs, wings or bodies of other insects and arachnids, sometimes in quite large and spectacular numbers, looking like bright red beads.

Of all the desert's hunters, the most agile are the robber flies (Asilidae), which scoop up their prey in their bristly front legs, killing it quickly by plunging a dagger-like proboscis into the back of the victim's neck. Dozens of species are found in the North American deserts, the largest genus being *Efferia*, longish taper-bodied greyish flies with large, sharp eyes and a prominent beard and moustache, useful for keeping the legs of struggling prey away from the vulnerable eyes. Females robber flies often lay their eggs in the soil, where the larvae are predators on beetle larvae and other small prey. Many of the larger robber flies prey extensively on stinging insects such as honey bees, which seem unable to respond effectively with their stings. The males spend more time jumping on to females than ambushing prey, often without any prior courtship, although some species perform a little aerial ballet in front of the female.

Tiger beetles are sun-loving creatures, much at home in deserts. Although predators, and fleet-of-foot on their long spindly legs, they

Top: The prey of this *Efferia* species robber fly in New Mexico is a bee fly.

Above: Velvet mites are often seen in numbers after desert rains. USA.

Right: This gaudy but unnamed jumping spider male from Arizona has caught a grasshopper nymph.

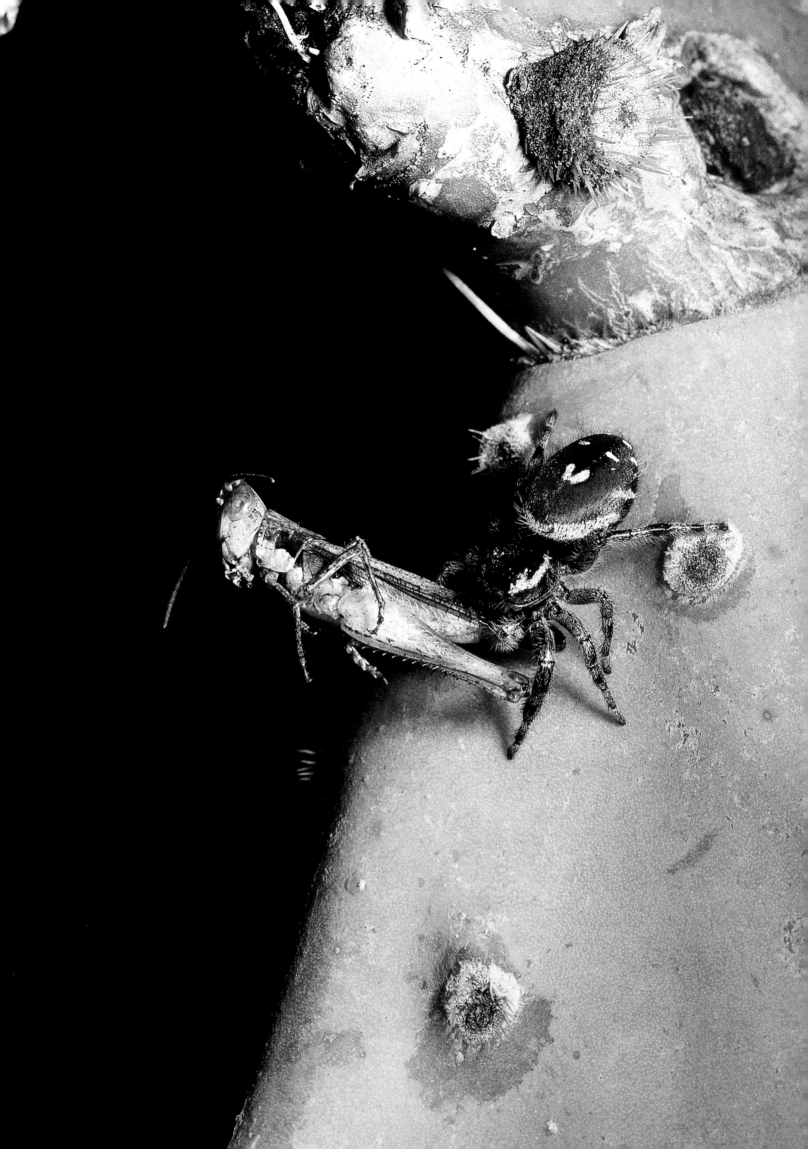

mainly seem to take small, easily subdued prey, such as ants, which are quicky torn to shreds with powerful sickle-like jaws. The larvae are basically all-mouth, with a huge set of jaws perched atop a skinny little body. They live in vertical holes in the ground, closed at the top by a lid formed of the open jaws, ready to snap up any passing prey. The average adult male spends a great deal of his time with his large jaws clamped tightly around a female. This constitutes a form of insurance, as once they have mated, the male needs to stay in contact until the female has laid her eggs in the ground. Even as the female prods her ovipositor into the ground, the male stays firmly clamped, ensuring that no rival can rush in and fertilise the eggs at the last moment.

As in any part of the world where there is sandy bare ground, *Ammophila* sand wasps are common in the American deserts. The females trundle back to the nest with a large caterpillar slung torpedo-like beneath the body. The living but stung and paralysed caterpillar is destined to fulfil an unenviable role as fresh meat for the wasp's developing larva. Caterpillars are hard to find in the arid regions, so some female sand wasps, particularly the *Ammophila*

abertii from the salt-flats of Utah, stay at home near the crowded nest-sites and 'mug' returning females, stealing their caterpillars. Furious fights often break out as the rightful owner tries to defend her property. Such larceny occurs in many sand wasps, as well as in other solitary wasps, such as *Rubrica nasuta* from South America, which catches flies. *Ammophila abertii* 'townships' are also the scene of desperate rivalry between males for access to the incoming females. It is common to see two or even three males stacked up 'piggy-back' on top of a single female, all struggling to be first to make a satisfactory connection with her rear end.

Below: Typical mate-guarding by a male tiger beetle (*Cicindela oregona*) in the deserts of Arizona.

HARMLESS DESERT FORAGERS

As dusk falls and the desert cools, hundreds of large, shiny, brown *Orthophorus* millipedes emerge from their day-time hideaways and climb up into the bushes to feed. Like most millipedes, they are not helpess when attacked, but coil tightly into a defensive spiral and release noxious defensive chemicals from pores along the sides of the body. Nightfall is also the time for many caterpillars to stir themselves from their day-time resting places. The California tent caterpillar (*Malacosoma californicum*) spends the day in invulnerable hairy masses on broad silken tents that are constructed using silk glands in the mouthparts. They often gang up on their plant hosts to such an extent that a whole grove of springtime cottonwoods in a desert gulch may be laid bare by their depredations. When this happens in a dry year, the tree will never recover sufficiently to leaf-out a second time, and dies.

The western deserts are relatively poor in butterflies, but some species are specialists there. The Mormon metalmark (*Apodemia mormo*) is virtually restricted to desert, as is the world's smallest

Top: The Mormon metalmark butterfly (*Apodemia mormo*) belongs to the family Riodinidae. Arizona, USA.

Above: These cottonwoods in Utah have been completely defoliated by thousands of tent-caterpillars.

Overleaf: At dusk in the Sonoran desert giant *Orthophorus* millipedes climb up to feed on the bushes.

butterfly, the pygmy blue (*Brephidium exilis*). Its caterpillars feed on members of the sagebrush family, which are so typical of arid zones from deserts to coastal salt-flats. Other lepidopterans are not so fussy. The white-lined sphinx (*Hyles lineata*) is found from coast to coast, in a huge variety of habitats. It is one of the few moths likely to be seen on the wing in the western deserts in broad daylight, where it hovers in front of thistles and other flowers. Its caterpillar feeds on a diverse array of plants, so it is not surprising it can find a home virtually anywhere, even in the arid southwest.

Hawkmoths or sphinxes visit many kinds of mainly long-tubed flowers, but some desert bees only visit one or two kinds. The little black females of *Evylaeus galpinsiae* are only interested in the fragrant white or yellow flowers of the desert's many evening primroses. As these begin to spread their fragrance into the desert air in the early evening, the bees arrive, and they're in a hurry, working at a furious pace before nightfall cuts work short. *Nomia* bees are also small and black, and nest in huge aggregations in salt-pans, hence their name of alkali bees. They work so hard and occur in such numbers that they are important pollinators, and where alfafa is grown commercially in irrigated desert, the farmers construct huge artifical trap-nests to encourage the bees to stay. Being able to forage without interruption is often difficult for the females of many bees, as they are constantly propositioned by ardent suitors. The males of *Protoxaea gloriosa* hover, legs dangling, beside flowers which the females are likely to visit, and viciously expel any unwanted visitors, even including tough-skinned beetles.

Above Right: California tent-caterpillars (*Malacosoma californicum*) on their silken resting tent in Utah.

Right: The pygmy blue (*Brephidium exilis*) is the world's smallest butterfly. New Mexico, USA.

Above Far Right: This white-lined sphinx moth (*Hyles lineatus*) is feeding at a thistle flower in Arizona.

Far Right: An alkali bee *Nomia melanderi* digging her nest burrow in Utah.

Only virgins are of interest to these males, so that females who have already mated are left to get on with their work in peace.

Once the bees have done their work of pollination and the flowers have developed into fruits, a fresh set of gatherers comes upon the scene, the ants. The industrious little workers of the western harvester ant (*Pogonomyrmex occidentalis*) are a common sight laboriously hauling along a seed much larger than themselves. Their colony's foraging-range encompasses up to 1,000 square metres (11,000 square feet), which will be defended against intruding workers from other nests, who will be killed. The nests are in the ground and well-worn pathways run outwards from them like spokes of a wheel into the surrounding desert, which is picked clean of seeds up to a distance of 30 metres (100 feet). Mating takes place in huge aggregations at special 'assembly points' to which the males and females of successive generations fly year after year.

Moisture is at a premium in the desert, and ants cannot tap plants directly for their sap, so they obtain it second-hand from aphids in the form of their excretions, known as honeydew. Aphids are relatively rare in the deserts, but where sufficient fresh growth permits a herd to flourish, they will be avidly 'milked' of their honeydew by the ants, especially *Formica* species. Some ants actually herd their aphids, mustering them down into the nest for protection at night, and then shepherding them back up onto the plants next morning to feed.

Right: The female of *Protoxaea gloriosa* is a handsome bee.

Far Right: In a very arid region of Utah, *Formica* red ants 'milk' aphids on one of the few annual plants to be seen in a dry springtime.

Below: Western harvester ants (*Pogonomyrmex occidentalis*) taking seeds to their nest in New Mexico.

FLIES WITH UNPLEASANT HABITS

A furry brown fly, rather like a small bumble bee, hovering in front of a desert flower may look innocuous, and so too does a plump black fly sitting on a sun-drenched stone, but they both have a secret and rather murky past. The furry fly will be one of several kinds of bee flies (Bombyliidae) that are found in many habitats, but are most at home in deserts. *Bombylius* and *Systoechus* are both brown furry flies, but the former tend to be rather bigger. The females hover above the entrance-holes leading down into solitary bees' nests, and 'bomb' their eggs into them. The egg hatches into a huge-jawed larva that makes its way down into the nest-burrow and kills the resident bee larva. This eliminates any competition for the store of food laid down for the rightful occupant, now deceased. Some species of *Systoechus* parasitise the egg-pods of locusts, while the darker-bodied, less furry species of *Anthrax* are mainly parasites of beetle larvae, including the formidable mega-mouth larvae of the tiger beetles. The female *Anthrax* lays her eggs in the ground near to a host, and the larva makes its own way towards its living meal.

Eulonchus looks like a miniature version of *Systoechus*, but belongs to the family Acroceridae, whose members also have gruesome larval habits. The females lay huge numbers of eggs in prominent places. Sometimes several females gather in the same spot, so that huge mounds of eggs are amassed. The tiny but highly mobile larva has about one week in which to seek out a spider, after which it dies. A successful larva enters the spider's body and feeds within, emerging to pupate from the body of the doomed host.

A large, fat fly on a stone on a desert hilltop will probably be a male bot fly (Cuterebridae) waiting for a female. The females fly to these hilltops specifically to mate. Bot fly larvae develop inside mammals, such as wood rats or rabbits. The large female lays her eggs directly on the rabbit's body, and the larva either bores its way into the skin, or enters via a natural opening. It then makes its way through the rabbit's tissues, ending up just beneath the skin. It pierces a small hole in the skin for breathing purposes, through which it eventually emerges to drop to the ground and pupate.

Left: Like all acrocerid flies, this *Eulonchus* from Utah develops as an internal parasite of spiders.

Above: A *Cuterebra* male 'hilltopping' in Arizona.

Above: Most *Anthrax* bee flies are not hairy. This mating pair is *A. seriepunctata* from the Chihuahuan desert in Mexico.

Left: This *Systoechus* from Utah is a typically hairy bee fly.

Below: Shuffling across the dry ground of the Chihuahuan desert in Mexico, an *Anthrax acroleuca* bee fly lays her eggs.

MIDDLE-EASTERN DESERTS

The Middle East is a meeting point for the deserts of North Africa and Asia, forming a melting pot of 'bugs' from both regions, plus a large number which are endemic to the Middle East itself. In order to get a flavour of the region, we propose to take a walk in early spring through a desert region in Israel, and describe the 'bugs' observed over a period of about two hours.

Much of Israel is a barren-looking vista of bare rock, scree and sand. In dry years there can be little to see, but after reasonably good winter rains there is a modest flush of vegetation that brings about a renaissance in the insect life. This year the rains have been quite good, and there are thousands of small seedling plants scattered across the desert landscape. Few of these will ever grow up, as they are being slaughtered by thousands of hairy brown caterpillars of the moth *Ochogyna loewii*, a member of the Arctiidae. Like most furry arctiid caterpillars, these will cause a long-lasting urtication (a stinging sensation) if handled. The handful of fortunate

Right: The arid landscape of eastern Israel.

Below: *Ochogyna loewii* moth caterpillars.

seedlings missed by the caterpillars are being grazed down by the strangest-looking beetle of this desert, the three-toothed darkling beetle (*Sepidium tricuspidatum*). The knobbly exterior of this floury beetle blends perfectly into the mealy-white ground, and its armour would be a tough nut to crack for any predator. Several large black darkling beetles are lumbering around, and one of these, a *Pimelia* of some kind, spends several frustrating minutes fruitlessly trying to tear open the tough silken case of a bagworm moth caterpillar (Psychidae), whose bag is festooned with bits of dead grass. The caterpillar withdraws into the safety of its bag, and its tough silk proves resistant to the beetle's best efforts. Nearby several more bagworms, are hauling their clumsy homes through the fuzz of grass and young seedlings that mark a winter-time puddle of water. Here too a few wild flowers are in bloom, proving irresistible to several kinds of blister beetles whose bold markings warn of an ability to ooze a caustic and irritating liquid when provoked, which can blister human skin. In some species the larvae develop in grasshopper egg-pods, in others the larva hitches a ride on a bee returning to its nest, where the beetle larva develops as a parasite. Not all the flowers sport blister beetles, however, one has a *Trichodes affinis* bee

wolf beetle (Cleridae) resplendent in its warning uniform of black and red bands. It looks remarkably similar to the hordes of black and red burnet moths (*Zygaena graslini*) that have gathered nearby on a carpet of flowers, and this could be an example of mimicry

Little puffs of dust sprout up from our toes as we walk along, and then suddenly a buzz comes form one of the puffs and a wasp is hovering near our knees. We stand still, and the wasp calms down and lands on a rock near our feet. Now we see that we had been just about to tread on the wasp in the middle of building its little volcano-shaped mud nest, for this is a potter wasp, a skilled artisan with clay. By filling its crop with water at a distant source, the wasp can make its own mortar on site, mixing the water with dust to form an easily-worked and very malleable building material. When each nest is finished, the wasp fills it with several paralysed caterpillars and then lays an egg, which is suspended from the roof of the nest on a thread, leaving it hanging just above the topmost caterpillar. When the tiny larva hatches, it will cling on to its egg-shell with its tail while reaching down to start eating the first caterpillar, which, being still capable of some movement, could damage or kill the fragile larva if it were actually sitting on top of its food store.

Top: Bagworm moth caterpillar dragging its home across the desert floor.

Above: *Mylabris scabiosa* is one of many colourful blister beetles found in the deserts of the Middle East.

Above Left: *Pimelia* darkling beetle attacking a bagworm.

Top, Centre and Above: With delicate precision a *Delta dimidiatipenne* potter wasp adds a lip to her nest (**Top**). With the nest completed, the potter wasp stocks it with small caterpillars (**Centre**), then lays an egg inside and seals it up with mud (**Above**).

Left: This bee-wolf beetle *Trichodes affinis* may be a Müllerian mimic of burnet moths, such as *Zygaena graslini*.

3 BUGS IN GRASSLANDS

The world's areas of natural grasslands are now much diminished.

If you take a flight from Buenos Aires to Cordoba in Argentina, and look down on what used to be endless vista of rolling grasslands, the pampa, all you now see is a checkerboard of cultivated fields. The vast North American prairies have suffered likewise, and have largely disappeared, along with their 'bugs'. Much of Europe's best natural grassland is in mountains, while lowland grasslands are largely artefacts produced by centuries of traditional farming methods, most of which are also now in decline, along with all the attendant wildlife. Many grassland 'bugs' now survive only on clifftops, roadsides, or waste areas, but where traditional hay meadows and sheep-grazed pastures still survive, often in reserves, they still support a wide range of grassland bugs. Moors and heaths also support many typical grassland insects, and are particularly well represented in the British Isles.

The last really great areas of natural grasslands still surviving more or less intact are the savannas of eastern and southern Africa. Strictly speaking much of this area is not pure grassland, which is best represented on the Serengeti plains of Tanzania. Most savanna is a mixture of

Left: Black-veined white butterflies (*Aporia crataegi*) roosting in long grass. Europe.

Right: *Macrotermes* termite mound with its 2.5-metre (eight-foot) high chimney in Kenya.

woodland, semi-open bushland and open grassy plains, dissected by rivers bordered by dense gallery forest. In central Brazil there is a huge savanna-like area called the campo cerrado, which is more or less the South American equivalent of the African savannas, but without all the 'big game' animals. The campo cerrado has developed on very poor soils, but a way has now been developed to enrich these, and in recent years vast areas of the campo cerrado have been destroyed in order to grow soya bean, and the myriad fascinating 'bugs' that lived there are no more.

Above Left: In the British Isles the silver-spotted skipper butterfly (*Hesperia comma*) prefers grassland on chalk hills.

Above: The clouded yellow butterfly (*Colias croceus*) seen here mating in open grassland, is a noted migrant. Europe.

Left: Damselflies often migrate locally into nearby grasslands to mate. These are blue-tailed damselflies (*Ischnura elegans*) from Europe.

Above Right: The poplar hawk moth (*Laothoe populi*) often breeds on sallow bushes in grassy heathland. England.

Right: The warningly coloured caterpillar of the spurge hawk moth (*Hyles euphorbiae*) on a grassy Italian hillside.

Overleaf: The emperor moth (*Saturnia pavonia*) is found on grassy heaths and moors in Europe.

Bugs of the African Savannas

In East Africa the savanna is often fairly open, although well blessed with large numbers of acacia trees, which often occur in dense groves. In most of southern Africa the savanna is more like a kind of open woodland, dominated over huge areas by the mopane tree (pronounced mow-paan-ee). In the long dry season typical of the African savannas most of the 'bugs' disappear, only to appear in numbers soon after the first rains. Some of the butterflies even have different dry and wet season colours, which make them look like completely different species. In the gaudy commodore (*Junonia octavia*), for example, the dry season form is reddish-orange, while the wet season form is bright blue with scarlet spots. It seems that it is temperature during the caterpillar's life that determines which form of adult is eventually produced; when it is cool, then a dry-season form will result, if warmer, then the wet-season form emerges.

The most conspicuous and permanent evidence that 'bugs' are present in plenty are the countless termite mounds that often stud

Right: Acacias in Kenyan savanna country.

Below: *Gasteroclisus* weevil in Kenyan savanna.

Right: The yellow patch covering the top of the thorax of this male *Xylocopa nigra* carpenter bee in Kenya indicates that he has been making repeated visits to large legume flowers. On younger flowers the anthers bend down and dust the bee's back with pollen. In older flowers the stigma takes the place of the anthers and brushes against the pollen on the bee's back, ensuring cross-pollination.

Below: *Acraea caecilia* is a common butterfly of the African savannas. Kenya.

Bottom: This eyed pansy butterfly (*Junonia orithyia*) is basking on a sun-dried heap of buffalo dung in Kenya.

the landscape. Dozens of species are involved, some building low, dome-shaped mounds, while others produce slim structures much taller than a human. Many *Macrotermes* incorporate a tall slender chimney, which provides natural ventilation for the nest below ground, drawing heat upwards very effectively. The amount of heat produced by an individual termite is, of course, tiny, but if you put your hand over the top of one of these chimneys, below which millions of termites are going about their daily business, you can feel the heat coming out. The amount of plant material that the termites harvest daily and take down into their nests is actually greater than that consumed each day by the huge herds of hoofed animals up above. The termites need all that grass to nourish a special fungus on which they feed—they cannot eat the grass itself. Their nests often give unwilling board and lodging to a host of uninvited guests, including centipedes, millipedes, bristletails, bugs, moth and fly larvae and even adult butterflies, which roost in the chimneys.

Left: The guineafowl butterfly (*Hamanumida daedalus*) is common on bare ground in savanna.

Below: In the scarlet tip butterfly (*Colotis danae*) only the male has the broad red wing-tips seen here. Kenya.

Above: The African monarch or plain tiger butterfly (*Danaus chrysippus*) is mimicked by several other species of unrelated butterflies.

Right and Below Right: The male and female of the blue-spot commodore (*Junonia westermannii*) look like different species. It is found in savannas and forest edges. Kenya.

Far Right: The wet season form of the gaudy commodore (*Junonia octavia sesamus*) from South Africa.

HEAPS OF DUNG

Below: This lion dung in Kenya has attracted masses of *Auchmeromyia bequarti* flies, along with some specimens of a *Hemigymnochaeta* species, both of which belong to the family Calliphoridae.

With so much grass disappearing daily down the throats of the thousands of antelope, buffalos, zebras and elephants that still thankfully throng the African plains, it is inevitable that a great deal of material is going to come out of the other end. This might be 'waste' to its former owners, but it is far from being that to a whole horde of 'bugs' that are equipped to recycle someone else's leftovers. Dung contains large amounts of highly nutritious material, although some kinds are more valuable than others. Elephants eat large amounts of tree bark and other tough indigestible food, so their dung is very fibrous and is only attractive to some of the more robust dung beetles. Buffalo dung is less fibrous and more easily worked, and is much sought after by beetles and flies. In fact the competition is so intense that there is often a race to get there first before someone else grabs all the goodies, and fights over ownership often develop.

Some of the dung beetles bury caches of dung directly beneath the supply-heap. Others try to remove their share from the over-crowded vicinity by fashioning the raw dung into neat balls. These are then rolled away and buried as a food supply for the beetles' larvae. Without this rapid waste-disposal service, the savannas would soon become clogged with heaps of rock-hard dung, killing the grasses and eventually starving out the large grazing animals themselves. So in a way, the dung beetles and their co-workers are as responsible for the survival of the buffaloes as the buffaloes are for the survival of their tiny allies.

Right, Top to Bottom: A fight sequence in a Kenyan dung-rolling beetle. In an effort to remove as much fresh buffalo dung as possible before the competition took it all, this *Scarabaeus aeratus* had made a dung ball which was much too large to handle and could only be moved with great effort. Attracted by this, a second beetle mounted the huge ball and started to carve away part of one side. Quite a large lump had been detached before the rightful owner noticed what had happened, and came across to investigate. A fight broke out, during which the owner, having the advantage of the high ground on top of its ball, was able to flip its adversary over on to its back several times, although on one or two occasions the intruder was able to drag its rival over on to its back as well. After several minutes of fighting, the original owner gave up, went back to its remaining portion of the original ball and formed it into a more manageable ball, which it then rolled off easily. Meanwhile the intruder formed its spoils into a ball and duly removed it from the scene of battle at great speed.

Below: This *Orthochtha dasycnemis* grasshopper has chosen to lay her eggs in the bare rain-softened ground of a path in Kenyan savanna.

Bottom: This *Thomisus* crab spider is standing guard over her eggs on a palm leaf in Kenyan savanna. The females do not usually survive to see their babies hatch.

Right: The ootheca of this large *Polyspilota aeruginosa* mantis is almost complete, and she is just adding the last few drops of frothy coating. Uganda.

Grasshoppers also need fresh grass, so they too owe much to the waste-disposal gangs. Most grasshoppers lay their eggs in the ground, often choosing a sandy spot which can be easily penetrated by the tip of the female's abdomen. She probes down with this, eventually extending her telescopic abdominal segments well below the surface into the cooler zone beneath. She then lays 50-100 eggs, and for additional protection these are bathed in a liquid which soon hardens to form a tough protective casing. These egg-pods hatch when the rains come and there is plenty of tender fresh grass for the tiny young nymphs to feed on.

In most praying mantises the eggs are laid in the open, often in some prominent place on a twig, fence post or grass stem. The larger species such as *Polyspilota aeruginosa* make a basket-shaped pod, known as an ootheca, in which the eggs in the centre are covered in a layer of foam. This hardens to form a spongy and very durable papery layer that is very resistant to weather and many enemies, although it is easily penetrated by the needle-like ovipositor of tiny, black, parasitic wasps that soon find the fresh ootheca, laying their own small eggs within the much larger mantis eggs. Having a

keen-eyed guard would prevent this, and in many smaller mantises, such as *Galepsus*, *Oxyophthalmellus* and *Tarachodula*, this is exactly what happens. The wingless females lay down their ootheca in the form of a flat, extended mat cemented to a leaf or stem. The female is able to cover the ootheca quite adequately with her body, and she sits over it until the babies hatch. She can protect the eggs against all-comers, such as parasitic wasps, assassin bugs and spiders. In fact many spiders also act in a similar way; female crab spiders, for example, can often be found on watch atop their white egg-sacs.

In most 'bugs' it is the females who stay and guard the eggs, but in at least two African assassin bugs, *Rhinocoris iracundus* and *Rhinocoris tristis*, it is the males who perform this task. They make efficient guardians and will assiduously drive away tiny parasitic wasps who try to attack the eggs. Males on sentry-duty are extremely attractive to egg-laden females, who are quite pushy in

their attempts to add more eggs to the male's clutch. Naturally the male insists on mating before he allows her to start laying, as otherwise he could find himself looking after another male's offspring. In this species 'winner takes all' and the last male to mate fathers all or most of the offspring, regardless of whether or not the female mated earlier with a different male.

Solitary wasp females do not generally stay to guard their eggs or offspring, but do put in a deal of hard work to give their progeny the best possible start in life. Spider-hunting wasps (Pompilidae), for example, can often be seen dragging a paralysed spider across the burning ground. Mud-dauber wasps belong to a different family, but also capture spiders, which are placed inside a neat mud nest plastered against a tree, rock or building. The large sphecid wasp (*Sphex tomentosus*) takes katydids, often quite leaf-like varieties that the female wasp apparently has no trouble in detecting among

Above Left: The tiny black wasp creeping towards this *Rhinocoris tristis* assassin bug male will try to lay her eggs within the batch he is guarding. However, he is supremely vigilant, and repeatedly drives her away. Kenya.

Above: Mud-dauber wasps, such as this *Sceliphron spirifex* from Kenya, collect their building material from the edges of puddles and ponds.

Left: Like most pompilid wasps, *Batozonellus fuliginosus* from Kenya catches spiders.

Below: A *Sphex tomentosus* hunting wasp dragging a paralysed katydid to her nest in Kenya.

Right: A *Podalonia* sand wasp struggles to keep her footing as she heaves a large caterpillar up a steep bank beside a river in Kenya.

Below Right: The nests of the social wasp *Belonogaster juncea* are usually attached to bushes in savannas. Kenya.

genuine foliage. Sand wasps (*Ammophila* and *Podalonia*) are as common in the African savannas as they often are in European or North American grasslands and sand dunes. The nest-bound females move in spurts across the ground, burdened down by bulky and very heavy caterpillars, which will furnish their offspring with all the food they need in one giant helping. Some sand wasps capture smaller caterpillars, providing a regular supply of these as and when the larva runs short of food, as determined by the female during regular status-checks. All these wasp larvae are careful not to kill their living but helpless fodder before its use is nearly at an end, otherwise it would soon go mouldy and be useless.

The more advanced wasps are social, and make paper nests in which the young inhabit individual cells. The adults feed the larvae on a diet of chewed-up 'bugs' on a regular basis, rather than shoving one huge intact meal into the cell. *Belonogaster* are among the most primitive of social wasps, in that all the females in a nest lay eggs as equals, so there is no bossy queen monopolising all the egg-laying, which is the undemocratic norm in most other social wasps.

SAVANNA ANTS

Bushes and trees in the savannas often bear the green pouch-like nests of the weaver ant (*Oecophylla longinoda*). The nests are formed by binding together the living green leaves, using larval silk. The nests eventually start to fall apart as the silk ages and the leaves go brown. Then the whole nest packs up and leaves for a new home, all the larvae and pupae being carried by the adults in a massive transloca-tion exercise. Weaver ants mostly take small prey, which they overwhelm by force of numbers, often standing in a circle and pulling at their victim until it is torn limb from limb.

Another source of food and liquid for ants in the savannas is the honeydew secreted by various homopteran bugs, especially treehoppers (*Membracidae*). In the tropics these and other related bugs take the place of aphids as providers of sweet liquids for the ants, aphids being relatively rare in the tropics. The ants provide their 'milk' providers with a personalised bodyguard service, which is so good that in some froghoppers the females desert their young at an earlier stage than normal if ants are available as commando-style babysitters.

Above: These weaver ants (*Oecophylla longinoda*) are clustering around a small item of prey in Kenya.

Above Right: *Crematogaster nigriceps* ants enter their whistling thorn home through a tiny hole. Kenya.

Right: As a driver ant (*Dorylus nigricans*) column crosses a dirt road in a Kenyan savanna, soldiers stand guard all along the sides.

A rather small black ant, *Crematogaster nigriceps*, does not have to go to all the trouble of making a nest from scratch, but adopts instead a ready-made home. The whistling thorn acacia (*Acacia drepanolobium*) provides this free real estate in the form of huge bulbous swellings at the bases of the thorns. These swellings are filled with a soft pith which is easily excavated to provide a dry and relatively cool home. The bush also furnishes its tiny lodgers with a supply of sweet liquid from extra-floral nectaries (organs that secrete nectar) among the leaves, and with nourishing oil and protein from special outgrowths on the anthers (the pollen-bearing part of the stamen) of the flowers. The ants regularly 'do the rounds' of the bush, harvesting their free food-supplies and taking them to the nest. In return the ants' notoriously powerful stings protect the plants from large browsing animals, while caterpillars and other small leaf-eaters are disposed of very quickly. Similar ant-plant 'board and lodging in return for military services' relationships are found throughout the tropical world.

The most feared ants are the *Dorylus* driver ants, whose vast armies, attacking on a broad front, can scour a neighbourhood of every living thing unable to flee or else immune to attack through being unpalatable to the ants. There is a soldier subcaste with enormous heads and huge sickle-like mouthparts, whose sole task is to protect the other members of the nest. These huge soldiers stand on gaping-jawed guard along the edges of the marching columns, fearlessly attacking any threat that comes too close. Their nests are temporary but relatively long-lived bivouacs, usually excavated in the ground, and despite their painful bite, the ants are eagerly sought-after as tasty snacks, being eaten on a stick, kebab-style, by chimpanzees in some areas.

Right: Like many ants, *Myrmicaria eumenoides* will gather around groups of treehoppers (Membracidae) in order to 'milk' them of their precious honeydew. Kenya.

PREDATORS IN THE SAVANNAS

Left: *Parasphendale agrionina* is one of the biggest mantises of the African savanna. The young nymph, seen here feeding on a grasshopper, is slim-bodied and resembles a piece of dried grass. Kenya.

Below: Life-and-death drama on a small bush as this small mantis *Galinthias amoena* tucks into a plump fly. The mantis simply sits and waits on a leaf until prey comes close, than snatches it up in its formidably spined vice-like forelegs. Kenya.

Bottom: Like mantises, lynx spiders use the energy-saving 'sit-and-wait' style of catching a meal. This *Peucetia* is feeding on easy meat, a winged termite. These emerge in their millions within a few minutes on their maiden nuptial flights, providing rich and easy pickings for every termite-fancying predator within reach. South Africa.

Top: *Laxenecera albicincta* is a typically hairy robber fly, seen here feeding on a moth. The robber fly's proboscis is buried to the hilt in the moth's thorax, where the large flight muscles will provide a protein-rich source of food. Kenya.

Above: There are several species of *Promachus* robber flies in Africa, usually having beautifully coloured eyes. This Kenyan species is feeding on a hive bee, whose ability to retaliate by stinging did not apparently protect it from the lightning-fast pounce by the highly efficient aerial predator. *Promachus* is also found in North America.

276

CAMOUFLAGE IN THE SAVANNAS

Top: The grasshopper *Humbe tenuicornis* is perfectly camouflaged against the patches of bare ground between the grasses. When startled it suddenly dashes off in a rapid burst of flight, prominently revealing its bright yellow wings. When the grasshopper lands, the wings are closed and the grasshopper again melts into the background, thereby neatly confusing any enemy that had seen the flashing wings and was

expecting to see a bright yellow insect. Other grasshoppers have blue or red wings for similar reasons. Kenya.

Above: The lantern fly *Zanna turrita* (Fulgoridae) is well camouflaged among the rank grasses on which it lives and feeds. Kenya.

Above: After the frequent fires which tear through the African savannas in most years, many species of grasshoppers are able to turn black. Known as fire-melanism, this phenomenon ensures that the grasshoppers maintain their excellent camouflage, even though everything around them has been turned to shades of black and gray. Kenya.

Right: *Agrionopsis distanti* is one of several very slim, grass-like mantids. Kenya.

Below: The long, slim outline of this *Truxalis bolivari* grasshopper blends perfectly into the dead grass littering the ground. It has bright red wings.

Previous Page: After heavy rains the savannas are studded with wildflowers, some of which serve as killing-grounds for the mantis *Harpagomantis discolor* and other flower-like mantises. South Africa.

Right: Both the nymph (illustrated) and the adult *Lobosceliana* grasshoppers mimic dead leaves in bushy savannas. Kenya.

Below: With all the visual impact of a shred of peeling bark, a *Catasigerpes* mantis stalks her hesitant way along the branch of a small tree on a Kenyan savanna. When she froze in her tracks, the photographer looked away to switch on the flash, then took nearly half-an-hour to find her again.

Above: With its body held rigidly at right-angles to a stick, this *Disparomitus* ant-lion from Kenya looks persuasively like a twig. Ant-lions from many parts of the world adopt a similar posture.

Right: This *Odontogonus pallidus* assassin bug vaguely resembles a dead leaf, an effect that has been enhanced because the bug has chosen to sit on a real dead leaf while it waits for prey to come close. Kenya.

THE IMPORTANCE OF COLOUR

Above: With its bold warning livery of orange and black bands, this large millipede feeding on a bush in South Africa makes a far from tempting target for predators. Millipedes release extremely offensive chemicals from special pores on each segment, although some predators (such as primates) will rub a millipede on their fur, removing the defensive chemicals before eating it.

Left: Wasp-mimicry is rife in many insects, but none more so than in the clearwing moths of the family Sesiidae. This *Felderolia candescens* in South Africa as a particularly fine mimic of a *Polistes* wasp.

Top: As it runs around on the bare ground between the grasses of the Kenyan savannas this *Ectomocoris* species assassin bug looks just like one of the many black-and-white species of velvet ants (Mutillidae) common on the same bare ground. Unlike some mimics the bug is not defenseless, but packs quite a punch with a bite worse than many wasp stings. It is therefore a Müllerian (see glossary) mimic of the mutillids.

Above: Net-winged beetles (Lycidae) are extremely distasteful, have a very characteristic shape and colouration and are mimicked by many other kinds of beetles, and a few other insects such as moths. This *Purpuricenus laetus* longhorn beetle from South Africa is an excellent mimic, one of several different species in the same area.

Right: Responding to a gentle prod, this warningly coloured moth caterpillar from South Africa is rearing back and disgorging a blob of disgusting stomach contents from its mouth. Many caterpillars act likewise, and the fluids can have a noticeably off-putting effect when smeared on to attacking solitary wasps.

Top: The gaudy nymphs of *Phymateus* grasshoppers form large family groups in order to emphasize the warning effect of their spectacular palette of brilliant colours. Their odour is exceptionally obnoxious, and their toxic effects when eaten are quite traumatic. Kenya.

Above: The jewel-like *Callidea* shield-backed bugs are a shining example of warning colours backed up by an extremely effensive odour. Kenya.

Above Right: Blister beetles are almost always warningly coloured. This small *Coryna* species from Kenya is on a grass head in dry season savanna.

Right: The savanna flowers often suffer greatly from damaging attacks by beetles such as this *Coryna arussina* warningly coloured blister beetle from Kenya. Like most beetles, it prefers to feed first on the nourishing protein-rich pollen, before starting on the less rewarding petals.

Overleaf: The armoured ground cricket *Acanthoplus armativentris*, a species of katydid, has a dual defensive capability. Its heavily-armoured thorax provides initial protection from bites or pecks, buying precious seconds until an unpleasant yellow defensive fluid begins to leak out from the sides of the thorax and into the attacker's mouth. If the katydid is lucky, it will be dropped in a hurry, but some predators, such as mongooses, will crunch their way noisily through both armour and the rest, albeit with a look of acute disgust on their faces.

Temperate Grasslands in Europe and North America

Traditional lowland meadows are maintained by an old-fashioned regime of haying or grazing, resulting in a rich variety of plants and 'bugs'. On the hills, the grasses tend to be shorter, particularly on downlands covering chalk or limestone hills. In the British Isles such flower-rich swards provide some of the best of all grassland habitats. However, grassy open paths and clearings in woodlands also support many typical grassland 'bugs', along with those more typical of the nearby woodlands. Grassy coastal sand dunes are also very important for many species that can only survive in such open habitats.

The grasses themselves are an important source of food. Unlike in the tropics, where most grasshoppers seldom eat grass, the northern grasshoppers often eat little else. Even where grasses abound, not all grasshoppers are equally successful. The meadow

Left: Limestone grassland in the Cotswold Hills, England, the home of many typical grassland butterflies and grasshoppers.

Below: The Kiowa range grasshopper (*Trachyrachys kiowa*) lives in a wide variety of open habitats in the USA.

grasshopper (*Chorthippus parallelus*) can survive just about anywhere grassy, yet the rufous grasshopper (*Gomphocerippus rufus*), can only survive among short grasses on south-facing slopes of chalk or limestone. The caterpillars of many moths and butterflies eat grasses, especially the 'brown' butterflies, whose females often just scatter their eggs at random into the grass as they feed on flowers. Other caterpillars feed on the wide range of flowers that occur in grasslands. Many true bugs also live and feed on the grass heads, where their long, slim, straw-coloured bodies blend in well with the ripening late-summer seedheads.

Grassland flowers attract a variety of other insects, some of which, such as the leaf beetle *Cryptocephalus aureolus* specialise in one kind of flower. The common soldier beetle *Rhagonycha fulva* prefers thistles. Being warningly coloured it feeds quite openly, often in large groups made up exclusively of pairs engaging in what seem to be perpetual gang-bangs. Any spare male will probably be rushing around desperately trying to pull his rivals off their mounts, but they will hang on grimly as they must stay put until the female is ready to lay her eggs—only then will the male's genetic investment at last

Left: The buckeye butterfly (*Junonia coenia*) is common in open grassy spots in the USA.

Top: The meadow grasshopper (*Chorthippus parallelus*) lives almost anywhere that has sufficient grass, although it prefers a longer sward. England.

Centre: The rufous grasshopper (*Gomphocerippus rufus*) prefers short grasses with open bare ground. England.

Above: The hairy caterpillar of the drinker moth (*Philudoria potatoria*) eats long grasses in damper spots. England.

Top: Like most 'browns' the caterpillar of the meadow brown (*Maniola jurtina*) eats grass. The adult takes nectar from grassland flowers, such as this knapweed. England.

Above: The grayling butterfly (*Hipparchia semele*) lives on bare, open grassy places, such as sea cliffs, and grassy heathlands. When at rest with its wings closed, its camouflage is perfect. England.

Left: The American painted lady (*Vanessa virginiensis*) is as common in grasslands as everywhere else. The caterpillar eats plants in many different families.

Overleaf: The marbled white (*Melanargia galathea*) is a typical grassland butterfly. Europe.

get to be safely banked. They have few enemies, although some spiders will eat them, and the same applies to the black-and-red burnet moths that are such a characteristic sight on the summer grasslands. The black-and-yellow caterpillars feed on trefoils in the pea family, from which they absorb hydrogen cyanide. This makes all stages of the moths highly toxic, although at least one particular stink bug (*Picromerus bidens*) seems to relish them. Most spiders that bite a burnet moth quickly regret their impulsiveness, and end up 'vomiting' a dark fluid with every sign of considerable distress.

Pathways often provide perfect nest-sites for solitary bees and wasps. The tiny spear-tailed digger wasp (*Oxybelus uniglumis*), found

Above: Well-camouflaged on its food plant, a grass seedhead, the female of the meadow plant bug (*Leptopterna dolabrata*) is wingless. England.

Right: The boldly striped caterpillar of the broom moth (*Ceramica pisi*) occurs where the food-plant occurs in grasslands and heaths. England.

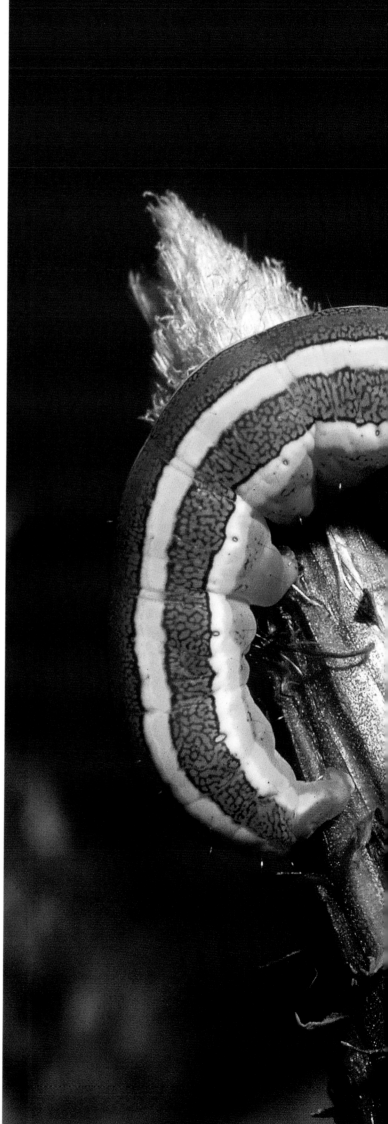

in both Europe and North America, catches flies and then carries them back to the nest impaled on the sting. The most amazing sight likely to be encountered is a *Prionyx* hunting wasp towing a grasshopper. Because these wasps often capture prey that is vastly greater than themselves, a female dragging her victim looks like a tiny tug boat towing a giant oil tanker. Subduing such large prey can be quite risky, as a big grasshopper can easily chew off bits that the wasp would rather retain in one piece! The grasshopper will also do its best to fly off, sometimes carrying the wasp with it, and will also bring up dark blobs of stomach-fluids to smear damagingly across the wasp's body and delicate wings. This likelihood is increased by the wasp herself, because she will always try to ram home a decisive sting in the throat, perilously close to the grasshopper's effluent-oozing mouth. When smeared, the wasp is forced to give up immediately and groom her body free of the unpleasant fluid.

Nomada nomad bees look confusingly like wasps. The females spend a lot of time flying up and down near the nest holes made by solitary bees, waiting to sneak in and lay an egg—nomad bees are

Top: *Cryptocephalus aureolus* is one of a number of leaf beetles usually found on yellow hawkweeds in open grassland. England.

Above: Thistles attract large numbers of mating soldier beetles (*Rhagonycha fulva*). England.

Above Left: The caterpillar of the gulf fritillary (*Agraulis vanillae*) eats passion flower vines. The adult lives in a wide range of habitats, including meadows and grassy field borders. USA.

Left: The field crescent (*Phyciodes tharos*) is a typical butterfly of the prairies and other grasslands in North America. The female lays up to 700 eggs.

Right: The burnished wings of the scarce copper (*Heodes virgaureae*) gleam on a grassy French hillside.

Top: Although one of the smaller species of burnet moths, *Zygaena fausta* is also one of the most beautiful. France.

Above: Like all members of its genus, the spear-tailed digger wasp (*Oxybelus uniglumis*) spears its prey on its sting in order to transport it back to the nest. England.

Left: A common sight on limestone downland in England—a pair of burnet moths mating on the female's cocoon, only shortly after she emerged from the pupa. This is the narrow-bordered five-spot burnet (*Zygaena lonicerae*).

Right: Typical warning colouration of red and black is openly flaunted by the day-flying narrow-bordered five-spot burnet moth (*Zygaena lonicerae*). England.

cuckoos and do not provide for their own young. The females find the host nests in an unusual way. The males, who hatch first (as in most bees and wasps), patrol up and down near the host nests and release an odour identical to that used by the bees themselves to mark their nest entrances. During mating the female nomad bee picks up some of this scent and it is likely that this reduces the risk entailed in entering into the host's nest.

Bumble bees are common on grassland flowers and some species need long grasses as nesting areas. In the small garden bumble bee (*Bombus hortorum*) the nest is placed on the ground, covered with a thatch of dead grass to act as camouflage. As in all bumble bees, this nest is started by a queen after emerging from winter hibernation. It may well contain uninvited guests, such as larvae of the bumble bee plume-horn hover fly (*Volucella bombylans*), which is found in both Europe and North America. The larvae are harmless scavengers, waxing fat on the refuse that builds up within the nests. The adults are very like bumble bees and occur in two forms, each mimicking a different species of bee. However, not all such lodgers pay the rent in such a helpful way. North American bumble bee nests may contain the far more menacing larvae of the cow killer (*Dasymutilla occidentalis*). The bright red wingless female searches out the nests and deposits a single egg beside each brood chamber. The larvae then feed on the bumble bee brood before pupating in their brood chambers. The adult female's sting is notoriously painful, hence the common name.

Left: *Prionyx* hunting wasps often take unwieldy grasshoppers much larger than themselves. USA.

Below Left: Nomad bees are cuckoos, and look more like wasps than bees. This is the yellow nomad bee (*Nomada flava*) in England.

Below: Some predator probably removed the thatch of grass that formerly covered this nest of the small garden bumble bee (*Bombus hortorum*) in a grass tussock. Most of the cells have been capped, but one (at top left) is still open and contains a larva plus its food supply. England.

The adult bees may also not always be as healthy as they look, and a certain percentage will harbour the larva of one of the broad-headed flies (Conopidae). Female conopids lie in wait beside flowers and engage in the somewhat hazardous occupation of ambushing bees and laying eggs on them. Bee and fly may tumble to the ground under the surprise impact, but the bee eventually flies away, apparently unharmed, yet destined to carry within its body the seeds of its eventual destruction in the form of the fly larva feeding unseen within. The fly larva may even change the bee's behaviour just before it dies, making it dig into the ground in a self-made tomb that will protect the fly pupa through the coming winter.

Left: Buff-tailed form of the bumble-bee plume-horn hover fly (*Volucella bombylans*). It is found in Europe and the USA.

Right: Following the act of mating seen here, the female of the broad-headed fly *Sicus ferrugineus* will lay her eggs on an adult bumble bee. England.

Below: Robber fly eats robber fly. A *Deromyia miscellus* has fallen prey to the much larger *Efferia interrupta* in a South Carolina meadow.

Above: Bees are ambushed by conopid flies while on flowers. This early bumble bee (*Bombus pascuorum*) in England is 'robbing' a flower of comfrey (*Symphytum officinale*), gaining access to the nectar via a hole bitten at the base of the flower-tube. By so doing the bee shortens the amount of time needed to visit each flower in the conventional way, but the flower loses out by not being pollinated.

Right: The low-flying amberwing dragonfly (*Perithemis tenera*) often skims across meadows. USA.

The most conspicuous flies on grasslands are often robber flies, which sit on stones or perch at the tips of twigs or grasses, waiting to dart out and capture a passing insect, which may occasionally be another robber fly of the same or different species. The larvae of most robber flies live in the ground, where they prey mainly on other insect larvae. Dragonflies are also aerial predators with sharp eyesight, and are often common hunting and mating over grasslands, wherever rivers or lakes lie nearby.

GRASSLAND SPIDERS

The common long-jawed orb-weaver (*Tetragnatha extensa*) is one of several similar species that like damp grasslands in Europe and North America. The long, narrow females often sit head downwards along a grass stem, and they are very difficult to spot in this position. During mating the male holds the female's jaws open with a special prong, and she usually lays her eggs in the open on the grass stems. *Xysticus* crab spiders sit around on leaves or flowers, and have fascinating mating habits. Before mating, the male walks round and round on the female, tying her down with a bridal veil of silk.

The garden spider (*Araneus diadematus*) is as abundant in grasslands as in woods and gardens. Balls of tiny yellow and brown babies clustered on leaves in late spring emerge from cocoons laid the previous autumn, before the female dies. By mid-summer the first males are adult, and trek off in search of females. They often cohabit with an immature female, making sure that they are close on hand when she makes that vital last moult and becomes sexually mature. Males will also court non-virgins later in the year, although this can be a much more protracted and risky affair, as the females usually have

Left: Before mating, the tiny male common crab spider (*Xysticus cristatus*) ties the female down with a bridal veil. England.

Below Left: Perched lengthwise along a grass stem, this female common long-jawed orb-weaver (*Tetragnatha extensa*) is very difficult to see. It is found in Europe and the USA.

Right: In springtime golden balls of baby garden spiders (*Araneus diadematus*) are a common sight in Europe and the USA. If disturbed, the babies scatter for safety, but soon come back together again.

Below: The male (left) of the garden spider (*Araneus diadematus*) is dwarfed by the female and can have problems during courtship. However, this female showed no signs of aggression and mated quite placidly with her suitor. England.

little interest in accepting another male. Before mating, as in all spiders, the male has to charge his palps with sperm, which he does by constructing a tiny triangular sperm web. He deposits a drop of sperm upon the upper surface, and then absorbs it alternately into each of his palps.

The wedding-present spider (*Pisaura mirabilis*) from Europe can reach very high densities in weedy, damp grasslands. This is the only known spider in which the male presents the female with a nuptial gift of a dead insect wrapped in silk, hence the common name. The female carries her large round white egg-sac speared on the tips of her fangs, so she cannot feed until the eggs hatch. This takes place inside a specially constructed silk nursery tent, and the female stands guard on top until the young have made their first moult and gone their individual ways. The North American nursery-web spider (*Pisaurina mira*) is very similar, but the males do not present wedding gifts.

Above: Male garden spider (*Araneus diadematus*) charging his palps with sperm from his tiny sperm-web. England.

Above Right: Vigorously jerking his silk-wrapped gift, the male wedding-present spider (*Pisaura mirabilis*), to the left, tries to evince some response from the disinterested but not aggressive female. England.

Right: This female nursery-web spider (*Pisaurina mira*) is guarding her babies, which are just visible in the folded leaf above her. USA.

A WALK THROUGH THE BRAZILIAN CAMPO CERRADO

Walking though the campo cerrado just after the rains have come is a fascinating experience. Everything is suddenly much greener, and there are 'bugs' everywhere. The air is filled with winged termites and queen ants, for both of which life is fraught with danger. The winged termites are a bonanza for many of the local predators, and are picked off in their millions. Sometimes they get no further than the bare brown mud walls of their nests, where we find prowling tiger beetles snapping them up, one at a time. We have to tread warily on the many patches of bare red earth, as hundreds of huge queens of Atta bisphaerica, the commonest leaf-cutting ant of the region, are valiantly trying to dig their nests in the rain-softened ground. We find one queen weighed down by a bevy of workers and soldiers, who are gradually tearing her limb from limb. She made the mistake of digging too close to an established nest, whose special

Right: The Brazilian campo cerrado starts to become greener after the rains have come.

Below: *Syntermes molestus* winged termites emerging from their nest in the ground, guarded by soldiers. Brazil.

Above: Both egg-guarding females and warningly coloured nymphs of the net-winged twighopper (*Aetalion reticulatum*) attract numerous ants.

Right: Easy pickings: an *Odontochila* tiger beetle snaps up a termite shortly after it left its mound for its nuptial flight.

Inset Right: After the rains, this *Cylindrotettix* species grasshopper changes colour from fawn to green.

nest-odour she lacked, so she was attacked and killed as a trespasser on private territory. There is no false sentiment in the harsh world of 'bugs'.

We walk through an area of last year's dead grass, and a slim *Cylindrotettix* grasshopper flips out from beneath our feet and settles itself head-upwards on a dead grass stem, where its straw-like tones are a perfect match. A little further on we pass through an area of fresh green grass, and find that here the same grasshoppers are all green, having changed colour with the rains to match the flush of new growth. This whole region is prone to dry season fires, to which the thick-barked trees are very resistant, and they usually survive, although with charcoal-blackened trunks. If the light brown bark-living *Trechalea* wolf spiders survive the flames, they also change to shades of black to match their newly transformed backgrounds. If they remained stationary we would never see them, but they are panicked by our approach and flip rapidly round to the opposite side of the trunk, where we can carefully watch them. It is pure luck that enables us to spot a large stick insect in a bush and, unlike the spiders, it remains motionless despite out close-up investigation.

Within days of the first rains, moths and beetles are quite abundant, and we find a succession of them sitting around on leaves. Many of the local plants have very tough leaves, so the leaf-eating insects need to be quickly on hand at the start of the fresh, more tender growth that follows the first rains. We are checking out every specimen of a particular plant in case it harbours the most interesting 'bug' we are likely to find here. At last we spot our first one, the large plump female of the sawfly *Themos olfersii* sitting hunched down over her batch of eggs on top of a leaf. This is one of only a few of the world's sawflies which exhibits such maternal

Left: Fire-melanism in the campo cerrado. This *Trechalea* wolf spider (*Trechaleidae*) has changed colour to match the burnt tree on which it lives.

Below: The elegant weevil (*Naupactus elegans*) is one of several members of its genus found after rains in the campo cerrado.

care, and she is warningly coloured, so the mere presence of her body helps to protect her eggs from enemies such as birds. If under attack, she will bravely stay put and buzz her wings in a threatening manner. She stays on hand nearby while the larvae develop and may even shepherd them to a fresh leaf. The food plant *Eriotheca pubescens* has very tough leaves, and only big-headed large-jawed baby caterpillars have the slightest chance of getting to grips with them. Making big heads requires large eggs and extended brooding times, hence the maternal care in this fascinating species.

As we approach a group of small trees, we see that the nearest are covered in thousands of adults and nymphs of the net-winged twighopper (*Aetalion reticulatum*). The females are perched awkwardly up on top of their huge egg-masses, each containing about 100 eggs. The sides of these masses are rubbed smooth where the females have regularly been sweeping their rear legs downwards, dislodging any tiny egg-parasites that may be creeping in with evil intent. Even so, the rearmost portions of the egg-masses, where protection is most difficult, have probably succumbed to parasite

Top: This hieroglyphic flower beetle (*Gymnetis hieroglyphica*) is keeping its head down during a thunderstorm in the campo cerrado. Its larva feeds on the roots of trees.

Above Centre: *Peocilopeplus haemophilus* is one of many brightly coloured longhorn beetles which appear with the rains.

Above: Speckled with rain drops, a female *Themos olfersii* sawfly stands guard over her eggs.

Left: Despite its large size, the walkingstick *Phibalosoma phyllinum* is not easy to pick out among the foliage of this small tree in the Brazilian campo cerrado.

Above: Lying flat on its side, the butterfly *Arcas imperialis* is surprisingly difficult to spot.

Left: Like most members of its subfamily (Arctiidae: Ctenuchinae) the moth *Eurota sericaria* is distasteful and warningly coloured.

attack. The nymphs are warningly coloured and form spectacular groups, mixed in with the egg-guarding females. To add to the family atmosphere, welcome guests in the form of ants are solicitously tending the bugs, giving added protection in return for sweet honeydew.

Butterflies are relatively scarce in the open areas, but among the trees we strike lucky and discover the little gem of a lycaenid *Arcas imperialis*. As we stand and watch it gradually subsides sideways onto a leaf, until finally its closed wings are almost lying flat, although its legs are still attached to the surface in their normal position. In this weird drunken posture it looks like a mottled speck of leaf, and we would be unlikely to notice it unless it moved.

4 BUGS IN TEMPERATE FORESTS

Temperate forests occur in North America, Europe, Asia, New Zealand

and South America. Both of the latter two regions are home to beautiful forests of southern beeches (*Nothofagus*), which are especially well developed in the south of Chile and Argentina. Australia is unusual in that most of its forests are dominated (often in huge single-species stands) by Eucalyptus trees, which host a whole range of special 'bugs' found nowhere else.

Bugs in European Forests

In Europe much of the woodland is fragmented into small pockets, often planted quite recently to replace more ancient clear-felled forests. Strangely enough, old undisturbed forests tend to be gloomy and relatively poor in the more conspicuous kinds of bugs as the forest floor is dominated by a carpet of dead leaves in which few wildflowers can survive. Fungi have no need of light however, and among the thousands of different kinds the stink-horn (*Phallus impudicus*) is especially interesting because it needs 'bugs' to spread its spores. Hundreds of flies are

Left: The Chilean rainbow ground beetle (*Ceroglossus chilensis*) is renowned for its iridescent colouration. It hunts other smaller 'bugs' on the cool, damp floor of the *Nothofagus* beech woods.

Right: A beech wood in southern Chile.

attracted by the terrible stink that the fungus produces, and eat the spore-containing slime that covers its cap, spreading the spores far and wide in their droppings.

In the British Isles the traditional form of woodland management is by coppicing, regularly chopping the trees off near the base so that they sprout a tuft of smaller branches. These light and airy coppiced woodlands are much richer in flowers and 'bugs' than darker unmanaged forests, in which you are unlikely to see many flowers much after the springtime spectacular when the trees have yet to leaf out and shade the ground beneath.

In woodlands managed for wildlife heaps of cut timber are left in piles to attract egg-laying females of longhorn beetles and other insects that breed in timber. The wasp beetle (*Clytus arietis*) is quite a good wasp mimic, with relatively short wasp-like antennae, striped wing-cases and a jerky wasp-like mode of walking. The European

Main Picture: An English oak wood in late spring.

Inset Above: Like many geometrid moths, *Neorumia gigantea* from Chile looks like a yellow fallen dead leaf. It is perched on a fern frond, not among the dead leaves on the forest floor.

Inset Below: Butterflies are scarce in the dense shade of the Chilean beech woods. This small fritillary butterfly, *Issoria modesta* is basking in a shaft of sunlight.

Below: The early thorn moth (*Selenia dentaria*) often rests on leaves in shady woodland, where it resembles a fallen dead leaf. England.

tapered longhorn (*Judolia cerambyciformis*) has many close relatives in the USA, and is often seen mating on flowers. Coupling-up can be fraught with danger for the male of many longhorns, who may lose a leg or two or a few antennal segments to the female's slashing jaws as she tries to throw him off.

Alder trees may be attacked by the alder wood wasp (*Xiphydria camelus*). The adult drills into the wood and inserts one or two eggs, along with some spores of a special symbiotic fungus stored in a special sac which opens into her oviduct. The fungus is vital because it can digest the cellulose in wood, and is in turn eaten and digested by the wood wasp larva, along with some of the infected wood. The larval frass (excrement) releases a characteristic odour, which

Above: The wood ant (*Formica rufa*) is found in very shady forest, usually under pines. The one on the right is taking liquid food from its nest-mate, a food sharing habit common in ants and many wasps.

Left: Flies busily feeding on the spore-laden slime on a stinkhorn fungus.

Right: Wood anemones (*Anemone nemorosa*) in flower in an English oak wood in April. Once the oaks are fully in leaf, they will shade out the ground.

Left: Having spent its larval life eating wood, this spotted longhorn beetle (*Strangalia maculata*) is enjoying a meal of dog rose pollen in a woodland ride in England.

Top: The wasp beetle (*Clytus arietis*) both looks and moves like its namesake. England.

Above: In order to insert the tip of her ovipositor into the bark of an alder tree the female *Rhysella approximator* has to stilt up high on her long legs. England.

is detected by the vibrating, bark-stroking antennae of a terrible enemy, the large parasitic wasp *Rhysella approximator*. Beneath its two centimetre (three quarters of an inch) deep barrier of solid timber the wood wasp larva lies helpless as the parasite's hair-like ovipositor is forced downwards and into its body, where an egg is laid. The parasite's larvae consumes its unfortunate host in just over two weeks, compared with the ten months needed for the wood wasp larva to develop—fresh meat is much more nourishing than wood and fungus.

Tree trunks also provides perching sites for camouflaged spiders and moths, although they are difficult to find and very widely dispersed. The leaves and fruits of the trees are more productive of different kinds of bugs, being more nourishing and freely available in the summer. Many kinds of weevils lay their eggs in acorns and other tough-shelled seeds, such as hazel nuts. The female acorn weevil has a long slim rostrum having a set of tiny mouthparts at the tip. She nibbles a hole in the acorn and then turns around and lays an egg in it. Weevils use similar methods to exploit timber, plant galls (abnormal growths) and many other kinds of plant substances.

Above: The mottled beauty moth (*Alcis repandata*) is well camouflaged when at rest on bark. Note how, in this unposed picture, the moth is not neatly arranged with its wings in the horizontal plane. England.

Above Right: The male vapourer moth (*Orgyia antiqua*) locates the wingless female by her scent as she emerged from her pupa in the ground and crawls up a tree trunk.

Right: After mating, the female vapourer moth lays her eggs on the bark.

The artisans of the beetle-world are the leaf-rolling weevils (Attelabidae). The female hazel leaf-roller (*Apoderus coryli*) first nips a leaf in several places with her mouthparts, at the same time rolling it up with her head and front legs. She 'sews' the finished article in place with a number of stabs from her rostrum, so that the tube she has created will not unroll. Then she places an egg inside this living cradle and the larva completes its development perfectly protected from the weather and enclosed by food. There are many kinds of such leaf-rollers, each with its own working methods. Some kinds

334

Above: This hazel leaf-rolling weevil (*Apoderus coryli*) is more than half way through her task of creating a living cradle for her offspring. England.

Right: Acorn weevil (*Curculio venosus*) showing its long rostrum. England.

sever the finished pouch from the tree, and larval development takes place on the ground.

Parental care goes a step further in the parent bug (*Elasmucha grisea*). The female lays a diamond-shaped mass of about 50 eggs on a birch leaf, and sits on guard until they hatch. If she is removed, all the eggs disappear within a day or two, mostly taken by ants. For the first few days after the babies hatch, she stands guard over them, but then they migrate to the birch catkins to feed. She shepherds them around as they grow, always staying nearby as guardian, and tracking their movements by a scent-trail that the nymphs leave behind them. Eventually she dies shortly before her offspring become adult themselves.

The caterpillar-like larvae of many sawflies also form groups of siblings, which are often warningly coloured. Many moth caterpillars are densely covered in stinging hairs, making them very unpleasant

to handle and leading to a long-lasting and painful rash in humans. Some of these caterpillars also use warning colours to advertise their ability to sting although some birds, such as cuckoos, can strip the hairy skin away and eat the succulent caterpillar inside. Caterpillars that lack both chemical defences and stinging hairs tend to blend in with their surroundings, often by mimicking a stick or twig. This ploy is also adopted, rather unusually, by adult *Phalera* moths from both temperate and tropical forests. The general pro-file of the resting moth is rather cylindrical, with the wings wrapped in tightly, and the flattened head chopped off short and covered with

Top: Cocking their tails in the air, these hazel sawfly larvae (*Croesus septentrionalis*) adopt a typical defensive pose. England.

Above: The hairy caterpillar of the sycamore moth (*Acronicta aceris*) from England.

Right: Parent bug (*Elasmucha grisea*) standing guard over her brood. England.

Below: The caterpillar of the vapourer moth (*Orgyia antiqua*) is defended by an impressive array of hairs and bristles. England.

Bottom: By lying lengthwise along a twig, the greyish caterpillar of the green-brindled crescent moth (*Allophyes oxyacanthae*) makes itself as cryptic as possible. England.

Right: Many geometrid moth caterpillars are superb twig mimics.

Below Right: The adult buff tip moth (*Phalera bucephala*) spends the day sitting on leaves, looking like a fallen broken twig. England.

an untidy thatch of yellow hairs, giving it a jagged look, like the broken end of a stick. It is often depicted as sitting precisely at the end of a real broken stick, with its head neatly placed above the shattered end, but these pictures are totally artificial and falsely portray the actual behaviour of the moth, attributing to it powers of site-selection that it does not possess. In the real world, the adult moths sit on leaves in the forest, where they resemble a stick that has broken and fallen.

Leaf-cutter bees use leaves not as perches but as building material. The female bee uses her jaws like scissors as she straddles a leaf edge and snips out an elongated segment. She carries this back to the nest slung close beneath her body, and uses each segment to build up a cigar-shaped nest-cell which she fills with a mixture of pollen and nectar. Then she lays an egg and seals the cell with a circular lid, always remembering correctly to cut this shape at the appropriate time.

Ladybirds are usually only associated with leaves when they are covered with aphids, which constitute the main prey of most ladybirds. However, some ladybirds feed on mildews on leaves, rather than aphids, trotting around and skimming the leaf's surface with their mouthparts. Certain 'bugs' use leaves as percussion instruments, utilising their fairly good resonating qualities as an artificial aid to attract a mate. The male of the European buzzing spider (*Anyphaena accentuata*) rapidly taps the tip of his abdomen against a leaf, producing a sound that is clearly audible to the human ear. In the oak bush cricket (*Meconema thalassinum*), a kind of small katydid, the male forsakes the usual katydid method of sound-production (that is, vibrating the wing-cases together). Instead he rapidly taps one of his hind feet on a leaf, producing an amazing volume of sound that carries far and wide through the night-time forest.

The oak trees inhabited by the calling bush-crickets are also filled with a maze of spiders' webs. Many of these are scaffold webs

Top: A large garden leaf-cutter bee (*Megachile willughbiella*) hard at work in an English forest.

Above: The orange ladybird (*Halyzia sedecimguttata*) feeds on mildews. England.

Above Right: Tapping on a female's lair, a male buzzing spider (*Anyphaena accentuata*) waits for a response. England.

Right: Male oak bush cricket (*Meconema thalassinum*).

belonging to comb-footed spiders (Theridiidae). In many species the female sits and guards her eggs until they hatch, while in a select few, such as the mothercare spider (*Theridion sisyphium*), the female feeds her babies mouth-to-mouth with regurgitated stomach-fluids—known as 'spider milk'. Oak leaves themselves—or at least dead ones—are mimicked by the comma butterfly (*Polygonia c-album*). With its wings closed the butterfly looks just like a ragged dead oak leaf, with the white comma-shaped mark resembling a hole with the sun shining through. The comma often basks on woodland edges, an activity that is important for butterflies who need the warmth to stay active. Certain 'whites' even have special basking postures that enable the wings to reflect the maximum amount of heat onto the body. The comma is one of the few butterflies to pass the winter as an adult, and is even more unusual in

Left: This female *Theridion varians* spider is guarding her egg-sac beneath an oak leaf in England.

Right: A basking comma butterfly exposes its tawny upperside, in contrast to the leaf-like underside. England.

Below: When at rest the comma butterfly (*Polygonia c-album*) resembles a shrivelled oak leaf. Europe.

Previous Page: The small pearl-bordered fritillary (*Boloria semele*) benefits from regular coppicing of woodland. Europe.

Right: Males of the European orange tip (*Anthocharis cardamines*) often search for females along woodland edges and open rides.

Below: The European brown hairstreak butterfly (*Thecla betulae*) prefers woodland edge habitats.

Bottom: The marsh fritillary butterfly (*Euphydryas aurinia*) is often found along woodland rides. Europe.

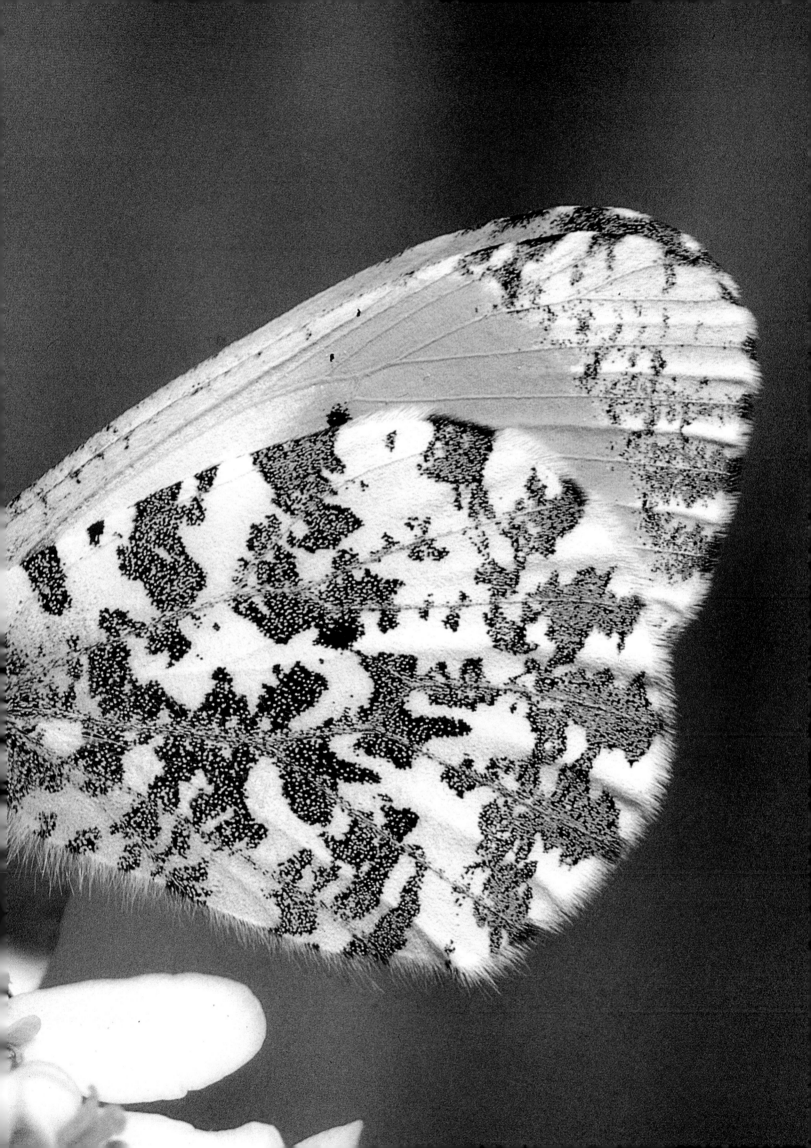

doing so in the open. Several similar looking species are found in North America.

Where woodland paths or clearings allow a vigourous growth of flowers and grasses, the 'browns' and other butterflies may occur in some numbers. The gatekeeper (*Pyronia tithonus*) and ringlet (*Aphantopus hyperantus*) are among many butterflies that are particularly fond of bramble flowers on woodland edges. Virgin ringlet females make their way to grassy, flowery glades where males are likely to be hanging out and 'offer' themselves to all-comers by sitting with wings spread in a specific 'come and get me' posture. If a passing male happens to miss this flagrant behaviour, she flies up and catches him, playing hard to get for just a few seconds in a brief chase before consenting to mate. By contrast, a female who has already mated skulks low and keeps her wings shut. Gatekeepers and ringlets are both typical 'browns' with small eyespots on all the wings, suitably arranged to distract a bird's attention away from the vulnerable body. Instead, a swiftly stabbing beak merely amputates a completely expendable scrap of wing, leaving the body to power the wings away from danger. In fact

Above: The white admiral butterfly (*Limenitis camilla*) frequents bramble flowers along woodland edges. England.

Above Right: A gatekeeper butterfly basking in the sunshine.

Right: The scarlet tiger moth (*Callimorpha dominula*) is active during day-time. England.

butterflies are still viable flying machines with truly amazing amounts of wing missing. Picking up a few pecks is not a problem for some of the day-flying woodland moths either, such as the brilliant scarlet tiger (*Callimorpha dominula*), whose warning uniform should keep enemies at a safe distance, without the need for the moth's potent chemical defences to be sampled.

A chemical arsenal does not work against all-comers. Ladybirds are usually avoided because they can leak their very bitter-tasting yellow blood through their knee joints. As well as tasting very bitter, this blood is also poisonous, and seven-spot ladybirds

(*Coccinella 7-punctata*) fed to bird chicks have been known to kill them. Yet all this is no obstacle for the tiny wasp *Perilitus coccinellae*, which lays its eggs on ladybirds. The wasp's larva develops in the living host, which still clings to life even after it gains an unwelcome hole in its underside as its lodger bores its way out. The larva then tethers the ladybird to the leaf with silk and pupates beneath the shield provided by its warningly coloured body.

Woodland paths with marsh thistles (*Cirsium palustre*) will often have their corresponding gall fly, *Xyphosia miliaria* (Tephritidae). Adult gall flies often have beautifully iridescent multi-coloured eyes and boldly patterned wings, which are constantly waved to and fro. The females stab a telescopic ovipositor into the flowerheads and stems of many plants, especially in the thistle family, which develop galls in response. In many species, including *Xyphosia miliaria* the males 'call' females by standing and pumping out a pheromone. In some gall flies the male spits out a rapidly-hardening column of froth on which the female is allowed to feed, but only if she mates with him first.

White flowers along woodland edges may harbour the common flower spider (*Misumena vatia*), whose squat white form harmonizes perfectly with its background. This very successful crab spider is common in both Europe and North America. It is not restricted to white flowers, but over the space of a few days can change to yellow, giving it a whole new selection of flowers to choose from. Like

Above: Ringlet butterflies (*Aphantopus hyperantus*) mating. England.

Left: *Xyphosia miliaria* gall flies mating on their marsh thistle food plant.

Right: This female foliage spider (*Philodromus aureolus*) has caught a fly on a foxglove flower. Minutes later the fly was stolen by the red ant seen walking across it. England.

all crab spiders, it has a fast-acting poison which knocks its prey out rapidly. Once it is feeding, it is impervious to further opportunities, and an insect can quite safely walk over its body without generating the slightest response. This is because crab spiders, in common with most free-living spiders, do not store prey for future use. Conversely, web-builders, if granted the opportunity, will go on a killing-spree until they have amassed quite a substantial 'larder' of stored food, all neatly trussed up with silk for future consumption. Unlike *Misumena*, the numerous species of *Xysticus* and *Philodromus* crab spiders do not choose a matching background, but often stand out conspicuously on brightly coloured flowers. Even so, they seem to survive and prosper without too much problem, and even a white *Misumena* will sometimes sit on a purple or blue flower and yet still catch plenty of prey. However, they are certainly more vulnerable to their own enemies when exposed in such a way.

Many woodlands contain ponds, and where these are shaded, they will contain little except a black carpet of dead leaves. Sunlit ponds will have an abundance of plants and insects, of which the most conspicuous will be the dragonflies and damselflies. These have interesting mating habits, quite unlike any other insects, for the male has accessory genitalia near the base of his abdomen, and it is to these that the female has to lift the tip of her own abdomen, in order to connect and form the so-called 'mating wheel'. One advantage of this strange position is that it is possible to fly nearly as fast as when solo, making the mating couple less vulnerable to predators. In dragonflies the male uses his anal claspers to fasten the female behind the head during mating, but in damselflies he clasps her on the top of the thorax, just behind the head.

Below: Fully occupied with feeding on a fly, this female flower spider (*Misumena vatia*) will not attack the honey bee feeding close by. England.

A WALK THROUGH A NORTH AMERICAN FOREST

Deciduous forests still cover large areas of the eastern USA, and also occur in the mountains of the west, often mixed with conifers. The variety of trees is much greater than in Europe, especially in the Appalachians, and it is here that we are going to take a walk through the forest, looking for 'bugs'.

The forest floor consists of a dense carpet of dead and decaying leaves. The process of decay is all around us, assisted in the first instance by bacteria and fungi, which begin the processes of decomposition, but are given a substantial helping hand by the micro-fauna of 'bugs' that teems in the soil and leaf-litter. Springtails and other small creatures live there in millions, while millipedes chew away at the dead leaves and help in the process of disintegration and assimilation into the humus layer of the soil. Most of the woodland millipedes are small, but in these forests there is a large and spectacular warningly coloured species, *Sigmoria aberrans*, that is active in the

Top: The millipede *Sigmoria aberrans* is common in the Appalachians.

Above: This caterpillar has no chance against a mass of *Aphaenogaster tennesseensis* ants.

day-time, and this is the first 'bug' we come across as we walk into the cool twilight beneath the trees. Above us, many of the leaves of the forest trees are being shredded by thousands of caterpillars, but they have numerous enemies who help to keep then under control. We stumble across a vivid example of this when we spy a squirming green moth caterpillar under an intense and fatal attack by an army of eastern spine-waisted ants (*Aphaenogaster tennesseensis*). They will cut the caterpillar into manageable pieces and carry them back to their nest in the ground, where the fresh meat will be fed to the ants' larvae. These are produced continuously from eggs laid on a production-line basis by the queen, and all fertilised by sperm stored after just a single mating on her nuptial flight.

On a stump we come across a new life-or-death drama. Another unfortunate caterpillar will not be eating any more leaves, having fallen victim to an eastern yellowjacket wasp (*Vespula maculifrons*). The wasp is busy using its meat-cleaving jaws to convert the caterpillar into a compact bundle that can be easily airlifted back to the nest. Adult wasps only take food in liquid form, so the caterpillar is destined for the larvae waiting back home in their paper cells. The worker wasps will announce that dinner has arrived by rattling their

Above: Eastern yellowjacket wasp (*Vespula maculifrons*) attacking a caterpillar.

Above Right: These two stink bug nymphs have nearly sucked dry a caterpillar.

Right: Delta-backed flower scarab (*Trigonopeltastes delta*).

antennae against the cell walls, whereupon the larvae will stick their heads out, ready to be fed.

The gloomy understory of the woodland is a favourite place for the large webs of two colourful spiders. The crab-like orb-weaver (*Gasteracantha elipsoides*) is a very spiny spider whose eye-catching colours probably serve a warning function. All members of the genus are rejected by a variety of predators, as is the second spider, the arrow-shaped orb-weaver (*Micrathena sagittata*). This, too, is abundantly spiny, and it is probable that these sharp and awkward protuberances are there in order to prevent the spider being swallowed quickly. The spines stick in the predator's gullet, giving time for the unpleasant taste to do its work. Once spat out, the spider will probably recover from its experience, as all these thorn-spiders have very tough bodies.

We pass through a sunlit glade where a question mark butterfly (*Polygonia interragationis*) is basking, wings spread. Its caterpillar has probably been feeding on the elms growing here. In the dense vegetation bordering the glade our clumsy passage startles several males of the black-footed meadow katydid (*Orchelimum nigripes*). The related and very similar-looking gladiator katydid (*Orchelimum gladiator*) is interesting because the males form singing 'choirs' called leks, designed to attract females for mating. The singers are real hustlers, and often engage in no-holds-barred biting and slashing battles to kick their neighbours out of the lek. The bigger males usually win and hold the prime ground within the lek, while the smaller ones are either banished to the margins, or are allowed to stay in the lek, but only as non-singers. Either way their sexual success is going to be zero, leaving the lusty big boys to pick up all the females.

Right: Black-footed bush katydid (*Orchelimum nigripes*).

Just past the katydids, on a sunlit leaf, another caterpillar has lost its fight for life. Shrivelled like a collapsed balloon, it is being sucked dry by a pair of stink bug nymphs. Predatory stink bugs feed on a wide variety of usually soft-bodied prey, especially caterpillars, although they are also adept at forcing their sharp rostrums through any chink in a beetle's armour. The bugs are too small to tackle a delta flower scarab (*Trigonopeltastes delta*) that is busy nibbling the pollen off a mimosa flower. Like many beetles, it is a destructive visitor to flowers. So are June beetles (*Cotinus nitida*), but the males we find in a struggling mass on the ground are not interested in flowers. They are after something far more important, a female who is just clambering out from her pupa in the ground, having spent her larval life feeding on the roots of a nearby tree. A June beetle female will only mate once, forcing the males to compete for her during the brief period after emergence when she is guaranteed to be a virgin. This leads to the formation of so-called 'mating balls' of wrestling males, a feature of various bees and wasps whose females also only mate once.

The scrum of beetles rolling around on the ground startles a female broad wood cockroach (*Parcoblatta lata*) who dashes out

Top: A trio of green June beetle males (*Cotinus nitida*) dispute the ownership of a newly emerged female.

Above: Female broad wood cockroach (*Parcoblatta lata*) with an ootheca protruding from the tip of her abdomen.

from cover and pauses for a moment in confusion on a fallen log. Projecting from the end of her abdomen is the ootheca, containing her eggs. She will carry this around until they hatch, a common habit in cockroaches. In some cockroaches the female carries her babies around, while in the bronze-hooded cockroach (*Cryptocercus punctulatus*) the young stay with their parents and form family groups inside galleries within rotten logs.

In shady woodlands it is common to see daddy-longlegs or harvestmen walking around, but today we have a bonus because we find one of North America's 200 or so species actually feeding on prey: a large fly. Harvestmen eat a wide variety of small animals, including caterpillars, spiders, earthworms and even other harvestmen. This is a surprise, as most predators shun harvestmen because of their stink glands situated near the bases of the first two pairs of legs.

Below: Harvestman feeding on a large fly.

Keeping to a well-worn path, we are startled by a brilliant flash of green as a six-spotted green tiger beetle (*Cicindela sexguttata*) takes to the air briefly before plunging to earth. Tiger beetles rarely fly, being fleet-footed surface predators, and this is one of only a few species that inhabit woodlands. The presence of the tiger beetle on the path draws our attention to a dark-coloured moth sitting quietly on a nearby leaf. It looks more like a net-winged beetle (*Lycidae*) than a moth, and is probably part of a mimicry complex with these distasteful insects. It is *Malthaea dimidiata* in the family Zygaenidae, known in North America as smoky moths as they are mainly dark and drab, rather than brightly coloured as in most European and Asian members of the family. By contrast, the ailanthus webworm moth (*Atteva punctella*) that flies out from our advance a few seconds later is certainly a good example of bright warning colouration. Like most members of the family Yponomeutidae, the gregarious caterpillars live in a silken web on their food plant, which in this species is a variety of trees and shrubs.

Flaunting its flashy colours is not the name of the survival game for the clavate tortoise beetle (*Metriona clavata*). It is only through

Top: Six-spotted green tiger beetle (*Cicindela sexguttata*).

Above: Looking like a leaf-blotch, a clavate tortoise beetle (*Metriona clavata*) sits tight.

Above Right: *Malthaea dimidiata* is a member of the moth family Zygaenidae.

Right: Red-spotted purple butterfly dry-puddling on a road.

long experience of hunting 'bugs' that we spot this tiny beetle on its leaf, where it looks like nothing more interesting than a blotch caused by disease—in fact this one is sitting right beside a genuine blotch. Tortoise beetles will clamp down tightly against a leaf when attacked by ants, preventing their attackers from getting a grip beneath the edge of the shiny carapace and levering them over.

As we cross a forest road we surprise a blue and black butterfly which flutters off briefly before settling back on the dusty dirt. It is a red-spotted purple (*Basilarchia arthemis astyanax*), and this male is dry-puddling, forcing fluid down his slender proboscis to dissolve essential salts in the soil, then sucking back up the resulting solution. When not dry-puddling, the males spend much of their time perched on prominent trees or bushes, waiting to ambush passing females.

The broad, sandy roadside is pock-marked with large holes, the sure sign of a colony of cicada killer wasps (*Sphecius spheciosus*), one of the largest and most handsome of all the world's specid wasps. The females dig large burrows in sandy soil and stock them with paralysed cicadas. In an amazing feat of agility the female wasp catches her victim in flight, where the clash of victor and

Above: Pausing near her burrow, a female cicada killer wasp (*Sphecius speciosus*) is unaware of the small grey *Miltogramma* fly that has rushed in to lay an egg on the tip of the cicada's abdomen. The fly's offspring will hatch first and feed on the cicada at the expense of the wasp larva.

Above Right: The big-eyed toad bug (*Gelastocoris oculatus*) looks like a pebble.

Right: *Actias luna* moon moth male in the Smoky mountains.

Overleaf: Green clear-wing skimmer dragonfly (*Erythemis implicicollis*).

Inset Overleaf: This green clear-wing skimmer dragonfly (*Erythemis simplicicollis*) is busy crunching its prey to pieces.

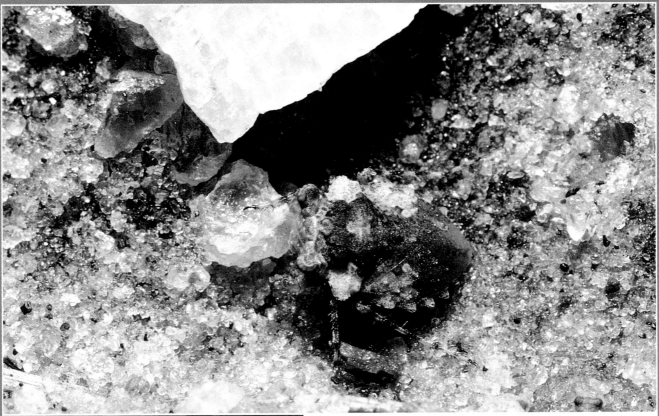

vanquished is marked by the pathetic squealing of the cicada until the wasp's sting sinks home and silences further protest. Unfortunately this wonderful wasp is often classified as a pest because it nests in large numbers on urban lawns.

The slope down from the road leads to a pond. As our feet scrunch on the waterside gravel a stone appears to sprout legs and run off. This 'stone' turns out to be 'bug-eyed' and is actually a big-eyed toad bug (*Gelastocoris oculatus*). Toad bugs live by ponds or streams and lay their eggs near the water's edge, in sand or mud or beneath stones. The adults often hop like toads, and have modified front legs for grasping small prey, which is located visually using the protruding eyes. Several dragonflies are skimming the water's surface, and these too are sharp-eyed predators, although they catch their prey in the air rather than on the ground.

We spend so much time admiring the dragonflies that by the time we head back homewards, dusk is falling and the first moths are beginning to stir. This is our lucky night, for on a leaf right beside the path sits a male luna moth (*Actias luna*). His huge pectinate antennae are fully deployed as they try to pick up any stray molecules of the sexual pheromone released by some far-distant female. Then he will

home in on her, following the faint scent-plume until he finally locates its source and acquires a willing mate.

We need a flashlight now and it soon picks out some silvery pinpoints of light glowing brightly on the forest floor as the eyes of a large brown spider reflect back the flashlight's beam. Her back looks rather fuzzy, and we discover that its is covered in a heap of tiny babies. We have found a female forest wolf spider (*Lycosa gulosa*) with her brood on her back, having hatched from a large white egg-sac that she carries around. The baby spiders emerge from their eggs and crawl onto the female's back, guided by special knob-shaped hairs that act as baby-grips. If they are accidentally knocked off, they can remount again quite swiftly by scrambling up their mother's legs. This hunter hides away during the day among dead leaves, emerging at night to look for food in the darkened forest.

Above: With her back covered in babies a female forest wolf spider (*Lycosa gulosa*) prowls the night-time forest.

Australian Dry Forests

There are more than 500 different kinds of Eucalyptus or gum trees in Australia, and these dominate the region's dry forests. A kind of rather open forest of smaller, crooked-stemmed gums is called a mallee, and has a characteristic fauna and flora. The stately mountain ash (*Eucalyptus regnans*) can reach 100 metres (330 feet) in height, making it the world's tallest hardwood tree. Eucalypt forests tend to be open, with scattered ground vegetation of flowering shrubs, but are often dominated by ferns in the damper forests. There is usually a thick ground-cover of dead eucalyptus leaves, which are slow to rot down, and are mimicked by some grasshopper nymphs and moths. While still on the tree, the leaves are packed with defensive chemical compounds, making eucalypts fairly immune to attack by herbivorous insects when planted outside Australia. However, back home the local insects have had millions of years to adapt to these defences, and thrive to such an extent that they may defoliate the trees over wide areas. The slug-like larva of the weevil *Oxyops scabrosa* is unusual because it eats the leaves in the open, rather than being concealed as in most weevil larvae. *Perga* sawfly larvae, locally known as spitfires, spend the day in dense family groups, splitting up at night to feed. If touched, all members of the group immediately jerk their heads and tails up and eject a blob of foul liquid

Above: The caper white butterfly (*Anaphaeis java teutonia*) is common in open mallee woodland in Australia.

Below: The domed webs of the hairy dome spider (*Cyrtophora hirta*) often occur in family groups of a mother surrounded by her offspring. This is particularly common in mallee country.

369

from their mouths. In the leaf beetle *Paropsis maculata* the larvae are harmless-looking little creatures, but they have defence glands that can secrete deadly amounts of hydrogen cyanide. The slug-like caterpillars of the various cup-moths (Limacodidae) that feed on eucalyptus have a different method of retaliation—they have spines that can inflict a very painful sting.

Right: A magnificent forest of karri (*Eucalyptus diversicolor*) in Western Australia.

Below: This katydid nymph is eating a *Melastoma* flower in a forest of mountain ash.

Bottom: With its close resemblance to a fallen eucalyptus leaf, the nymph of the grasshopper *Goniaea australasiae* is far less likely to be spotted than the fully-winged adult.

Top and Above: *Perga* species 'spitfire' sawfly larvae before and after they have been touched.

Left: An adult *Oxyops scabrosa* weevil on eucalyptus.

LOOKING LIKE BARK

Above: Fire is very much a natural part of the Australian landscape, and many fruits are so tough that only the heat of the passing flames will release the seeds. Many 'bugs' cope quite well with the after-effects of a bush fire, and none more so than the *Coryphystes* grasshopper nymphs, which quickly turn black to match the charred trunks on which they must now spend their days.

Left: This *Coryphystes* grasshopper nymph blends in well with the dark brown bark of the eucalypt on which it lives.

Top Right: Looking like a sliver of the constantly shredding bark on which it lives, this male *Ima fusca* mantis sits invisibly on a paperbark trunk in Queensland. After a fire, this mantis, too, can change to black to suit its radically changed circumstances.

Above Right: With its body pressed tightly against the bark, this *Cubicorhynchus maculatus* weevil resembles a natural protrusion on the trunk of a eucalypt.

Right: Unless it moves you are unlikely to spot this *Eurinopsyche* lantern fly on a eucalpytus trunk.

5 BUGS OF TROPICAL RAINFORESTS

The richest rainforests for 'bugs' are in Central and South America, but there is also plenty to find in the forests of the Old World. Madagascar's unique rainforests are very special because they contain large numbers of creatures found nowhere else, such as the weird giraffe-necked weevil (*Trachelophorus giraffa*) and the bearded weevil (*Lixus barbiger*). Despite their name, rainforests are not always permanently wet, and some seasons are often much drier than others, with little or no rain for weeks on end. During this 'dry' season some of the trees will lose all their leaves, but in most rainforests the trees shed their leaves almost constantly, just a few at a time. Unlike in deciduous forests, there is no mass leaf-fall every year at the same time, and this factor, combined with a rapid rate of decay, means that there is no chance for a dense carpet of dead leaves to accumulate on the rainforest floor.

Many rainforests have been disturbed by selective logging and surprisingly enough this often makes it much easier to find lots of 'bugs', which can be quite difficult to do in undisturbed virgin rainforest.

Left: *Myscelia orsis* (Nymphalidae) is one of the spectacular butterflies from the Brazilian rainforests.

Right: Rainforest waterfall in Uganda.

A logged forest will have lots of light-gaps, similar to those created naturally when a giant tree falls. When this happens many insects are attracted both by the fallen tree itself, to lay their eggs in its timber, and to the sudden explosion of plant life, which soon fills the gap with a riotous growth of vines and other vegetation. The ground-level of a virgin forest is often so dark that there is little to see, apart from a few specialised insects such as the South American glasswing butterflies, which shun the sunlight. In such a forest the bug hunter heads for a road or broad track that will act like a linear treefall, admitting light to the forest floor along a broad stretch. Rivers also admit light along their banks, leading to a so-called 'edge effect' with far more flowers and 'bugs' than normal.

Right: The bearded weevil (*Lixus barbiger*), one of Madagascar's many endemic 'bugs'.

Below: The royal blue pansy butterfly (*Junonia rhadama*) from Madagascar is found in both wet and dry forests.

Bottom: This male giraffe-necked weevil (*Trachelophorus giraffa*) was photographed in Madagascar.

Some insects thrive in the more open areas along rivers, such as the pretty Nisitrus crickets from Sumatra. Unlike most crickets, these are active during the day, when their intriguing courtship can be easily watched. The male first sits in front of the female and trills his love song. Eventually he turns his back on her and she creeps on to him, quickly nibbling at special glands on top of his abdomen. Suddenly he attaches his spermatophore (a bag containing sperm) to the tip of her body, leaps out from beneath her and turns around to resume his original stance. He spends the next 20 minutes guarding the female, waiting for the sperm from the spermatophore to make its way into her body. Finally he waves one of his back legs to signal 'time's up', whereupon the female bends and eats the now-empty spermatophore. The whole process is repeated several times until the female is fully inseminated and has also enjoyed several free meals of the empty spermatophores.

Contrary to popular belief, the rainforest is not filled with cascades of technicoloured flowers decorated with garlands of sumptuously tinted butterflies. Green and brown are the dominant colours of the rainforest understorey where mere humans are forced to tread, while any flowers that do occur are often disappointingly drab and tiny, although certain shade-loving butterflies

Left: Fallen trees, such as this giant in Brazil, create important gaps of light where many 'bugs' can be found.

Above: This low well-lit vegetation near a Sumatran river attracted lots of 'bugs', such as day-active *Nisitrus* crickets.

Above Right: A male *Nisitrus* cricket (left) raises his wing-cases as he trills to the female.

Right: Responding to the male's courtship, the female *Nisitrus* cricket mounts his back while feeding on secretions on its upper surface.

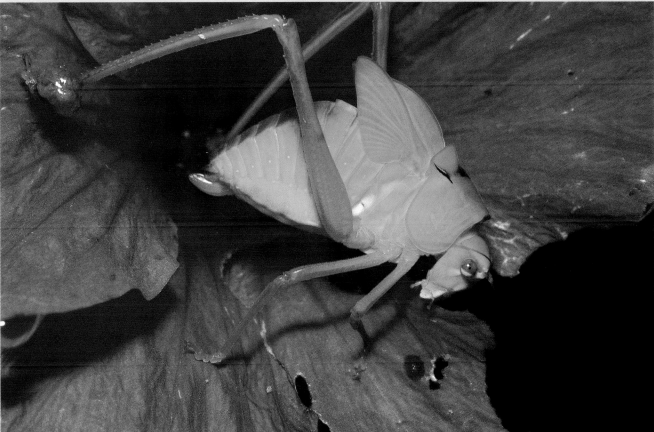

Left: The blue transparent butterfly (*Ithomia pellucida*) mainly feeds on insignificant flowers in the rainforest understorey. Trinidad.

Top: This *Acraea sotikensis* butterfly from Kenya is feeding on flowers in a man-made clearing in the forest.

Above: *Microcentrum* katydid nymph eating an hibiscus flower in Trinidad.

Below: Grasshopper *Cephalotettix pilosus* feeding on an *Ipomoea* flower along the edge of rainforest in Mexico.

Bottom: These tiny newly-hatched grasshopper nymphs have started to feed from the upper surface of a banana leaf in Trinidad.

Right: *Actinote pellenia* butterfly caterpillars in Trinidad. They benefit from rainforest disturbance where their *Eupatorium* food plant thrives.

Overleaf: *Anasa varicornis* bug (Coreidae) sucking sap from a *Cissus* vine in Trinidad.

may still find them. Many of the butterflies never feed on flowers anyway, but prefer sap, dung or rotting fruits, and those that do visit flowers are often rainforest-edge species which take advantage of the richer growth of flowers in man-made clearings and along roads. There they may be joined by forest grasshoppers and katydids which feed destructively on flowers, rather than pollinating them. Many herbivorous insects eat flower parts, which contain protein-rich pollen and nectar-secreting nectaries, offering higher rewards than mere leaves alone. Because they are long-lived, often surviving for many years, rainforest leaves have to be tough and durable and often contain anti-digestant compounds and other chemical defences. They may be easier to deal with once they have fallen and lost their chemical armouries, and the forest floor supports a whole brigade of 'bugs' able to make use of the constant trickle of material from above. The prime recycling experts are the termites, such as *Macrotermes*, whose blind workers harvest the dead material in bite-sized pieces, eat it and then use their droppings as a compost for the cultivation of their food supply, a special

Top: These *Zaprionus* fruit flies (Drosophilidae) are feeding on fermenting sap from a tree wound in a Kenyan forest.

Above: Fermenting fruit also attracts fruit flies, such as these *Drosophila* in Trinidad.

Right: Katydids have biting mouthparts, well-illustrated by this nymph taking large bites out of a fallen fruit at night in Trinidad.

388

fungus that is cultured on a comb made of dead wood in a subterranean nest.

Sap may be easier to utilise than complete leaves, and rainforests are full of large sap-sucking bugs. Damaged tree trunks sometimes leak large quantities of sap, which may start to ferment with a pungent odour that attracts many 'bugs', especially fruit flies, butterflies and scarab beetles. Fallen fruits will also entice fruit flies, as well as larger insects such as katydids and butterflies.

Some 'bugs' harvest miniature plant-life. Broad marching columns of *Hospitalitermes* termites are a common sight in some Asian rainforests, snaking their way down the tree trunks and across the forest floor. Each termite worker holds in its mouth a tiny ball of crustose lichens harvested from the sunlit treetops. As in *Macrotermes*, the columns of marching workers are blind, and follow scent-trails back to the nest. The columns are well-ordered,

with returning workers in the centre of the column and outgoing workers in the two outermost lanes, all guarded by an outer cordon of soldiers.

Muddy pathways often attract many butterflies, and sandy riverbanks—especially where animals have urinated—are also very popular. Dung is even more of a feast, especially when it comes from meat-eaters such as leopards and civets, and in Africa this will often be invisible beneath a rustling mass of butterflies, all pushing and shoving for the best place on the reeking pile. Only males are

Below: Flat-backed millipedes on a fallen tree in Costa Rica.

present, as they appear to require the nitrogen and certain salts in the dung to replace material lost when making the numerous spermatophores attached to females during mating. Even tiny bird-droppings prove an irresistible lure to certain rainforest insects, such as flies, alydid bugs and certain butterflies. Some butterflies, particularly members of the 'tiger-striped' mimicry complex (see below), of the forest understorey even accompany raiding swarms of army ants. The ants are followed by ant-birds, which snap up any panic-stricken insects dislodged and then missed by the ants, while the butterflies feed on the ant-bird droppings that occur all round the ants' zone of operation, simplifying the task of locating the droppings compared with searching the whole forest.

Wherever there are plant-eating animals, there will be other animals to feed on them. Some of the most conspicuous rainforest predators are the *Nephila* banana spiders, whose huge females, the largest of all orb-web spiders, inhabit equally huge and impressive

Above: African map butterfly (*Cyrestis camillus*) feeding on mud. Kenya.

Above Right: The mother of pearl butterfly (*Salamis parhassus*) is often attracted to muddy ground. Kenya.

Right: These blue triangle butterflies (*Graphium doson*) are drinking on a Malaysian riverbank.

Overleaf: This civet dung in Uganda has attracted many butterflies.

webs made of very tough yellow silk. The males are much smaller, and spend most of their time in the web of some female, where they constantly skirmish with each other for the best place in the web, near its hub where the female spends most of her time. The so-called 'hub-male' can easily slide onto the nearby female whenever he wants to try mating and is also conveniently close to her store of food which she keeps in a line near the hub. Although banana spiders mainly feed on prey much smaller than themselves, there is a definite lower limit below which they simply don't bother, and the males fall below that limit, so are rarely troubled by their giant spouses. Occasionally the webs catch very large prey, such as big cicadas and even birds.

Far Left: Banana spider *Nephila davicaps* female feeding on a cicida. Note the tiny male creeping onto the cicida's wing-top. Argenina.

Left: *Nephilegys malatanesis* feeding on a caterpillar. Sumatra.

Below: Dead-leaf jumper invading a web. Sumatra.

Nephila webs span broad open spaces between the trees, while some spiders, such as *Nephilengys* and many theridiids and pholcids build their snares around the tree-bases. *Nephilengys* males are also much smaller than the females, but relations between them are notably amicable and the male lives the quiet life of a squatter right beside vast bulk of the female. Relationships are even more permanent in the social spiders, of which several species are found in rainforests. The webs of *Anelosimus eximius* (Theridiidae) in South America are often huge structures that sprawl across several trees and bushes. They often catch large insects such as dragonflies, which would be too big for a lone spider to deal with. However, the big advantage of being social is the chance for co-operative effort, so the spiders rush out and subdue the prey together. The bigger it is and the more it struggles, the greater the number of spiders who pile in to help with the job of killing it. The communal spirit persists as the spiders start to feed, and there is no arguing as to who gets

what. The tiny spiderlings live in crêches where any female will regurgitate a meal to them on a first-come-first-served basis, so that mothers do not necessarily (or ever) feed their own offspring. The giant webs often contain caterpillars of the moth *Neopalthis madates* which live nowhere else and feed on the masses of discarded insect-remains that are always lying around.

In many Asian forests the resident spiders are at risk from a bizarre and highly-skilled assassin, the dead-leaf jumper (*Portia labiata*). Looking more like a dead leaf that has entered the final stages of disintegration than a spider, this amazingly intelligent creature will leap upon a spider in its web, perhaps having memorised its position first and made a complicated detour to get there. This sophisticated hunter will also lure a spider to its death by plucking a web in such a way as to mimic a trapped insect. The web's occupant trots down and falls victim to the waiting *Portia*, ending up as a meal, rather than getting one.

Top: *Acontista sp.* flower mantis feeding on a butterfly. Trinidad.

Above: Diamd's heavy jumper (Salticidae) feeding on a katydid in Sulawesi.
This is one of the biggest jumping spiders.

Left: Female lynx spider *oxyopos schenkeli* feeding on a butterfly. Uganda.

Many spiders do not build webs, but simply sit on leaves and pounce on passing prey. Praying mantises behave likewise but jumping spiders epitomise the active, sharp-eyed hunter well able to gauge the distance to their quarry and then leap upon it with amazing accuracy. Jumping spiders often tackle insects much larger than themselves, and cope with any resulting problems by dropping off on their dragline to hang in mid-air, where the struggling victim's feet cannot gain purchase on anything solid, evening up the odds considerably.

Some of the most interesting of all spiders are the ogre-faced or net-casting spiders (Deinopidae). These are usually quite scarce and hard to find, but in places they may be amazingly abundant, as in some of the Atlantic coast rainforests of Brazil. Instead of building a web and then sitting in it, the ogre-faced spider does things the other way round, it builds a web and then holds it. Of course, the web's size has to be greatly reduced, and it becomes an expandable net that is held at-the-ready, in a semi-collapsed state, in the spider's front two pairs of legs. When an insect comes near, the spider instantly pulls the net open to its full extent and casts it over the victim. When at rest the spider resembles a twig, and is very hard to spot when sitting lengthwise along a branch.

Assassin bugs are formidable predators and are often common and of enormous size in rainforests. They are sometimes accompanied by tiny black jackal flies that hang around waiting for the bug to live up to its name and kill something. The tiny loiterers then cluster around to refresh themselves on the liquids that generally start oozing from the prey as the assassin bug regularly stabs it with its rostrum, opening up a series of leaking wounds. Jackal flies will also sit on the backs of spiders waiting for a meal to arrive, and are found in temperate regions as well as in the tropics. The assassin bugs themselves mainly use stealth to catch their prey, but some South American species increase their chances of a successful encounter by rubbing their front legs in resin flowing from a damaged tree. The scent of the resin acts as a bait for stingless bees, which collect resin for nest-building purposes and fly straight into the trap set by the bug. Some very thread-like assassin bugs are specialists in moving around in spiders' webs without getting caught, feeding on prey snared in the web or on the spiders themselves. Assassin bug saliva is very painful when injected into a human finger, so presumably kills its victims very rapidly. The saliva then digests the prey internally, so that a convenient soup is ready to be sucked back up again. The prey is often carried around like a trophy speared on the tip of the rostrum, enabling the bug to take cover quickly if needed.

Left: Net-casting spider. Brazil.

Below: Jackal flies on a honeybee that has been caught by an assassin bug in Uganda.

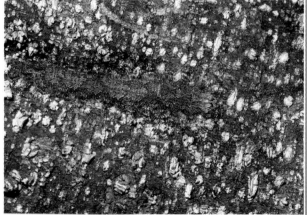

LIFE ON TREE TRUNKS

Above: Each of the world's tropical regions has its own species of large katydids that live on tree trunks. This is probably the best of them all, *Cymatomera denticollis* from Africa. Note how the colour and shape of the broad, wavy-edged legs, and the lobed outgrowths on top of the thorax all mimic the pale greenish lichens that are common on tree trunks and are visible on the bark close by. The speckling on the wings is designed to blend in perfectly with a variety of bark textures, and the wings are held close against the tree to reduce shadows, helped by the way the katydid presses itself closely against the bark. Eliminating give-away shadows is an important element in the camouflage strategy of most bark-living animals, including insects, spiders, frogs and lizards.

Above Right: Deletion of any shadows has been superbly achieved in two ways by this lasiocampid moth caterpillar in a Kenyan rainforest. Firstly, the caterpillar has settled its cylindrical body into a slight groove in the bark. This has enabled the broad horizontal fringe of hairs along the sides of the body to merge caterpillar and bark imperceptibly and almost seamlessly together. In fact, this works so well that the caterpillar was only noticed when it was accidentally touched, which made it jerk upwards. Despite this, several nearby caterpillars were covered in the pupae of a tiny braconid wasp, which had no doubt located the hosts using their highly developed sense of smell, rather than sight.

Above: A wide range of beautifully camouflaged assassin bugs prowl around invisibly on the bark of rainforest trees. This is *Euphena pallens* from South America, which bears a close resemblance to various *Carcinomma* species that occupy a similar habitat niche in Africa.

Left: Bark bugs (Aradidae) feed mainly on the fungal hyphae which infect the bark of diseased trees. The body is normally very flattened, enabling it to slide in comfortably beneath peeling bark where food is most abundant. However, some tropical species are often seen in some numbers feeding externally on fungus-infected trees and logs.

Below Left: Moths that spend the daylight hours on bark do not necessarily adopt a horizontal pose with their wings at right angles to the trunk. Many species always orient their wings vertically, as seen in this *Netis buteo* (Noctuidae) in a forest in Trinidad.

Far Left: Many longhorn beetles are active at night and need to spend the day without being spotted by their enemies. Some species are suitably coloured for living on tree trunks, such as *Ancylonotus tribulus* from Uganda. In this species the long antennae are held out to the sides, but in some longhorns they are bent backwards along the top of the wing-cases and held flat against the trunk behind, rendering them less visible.

Left: This South American walkingstick sits in such a way that it resembles the green lianas that often run up tree trunks like electric wiring, as visible to either side of the insect itself.

Below: This adult harlequin beetle (*Acrocinus longimanus*) has just emerged from a pupa within a dead tree. The large oval hole seen just beneath the tip of the beetle's body is a characteristic larval boring of this species. The adults are active in day-time, and are often covered in thousands of tiny symbiotic mites, which inhabit the larval feeding galleries and are carried to new sites by female beetles seeking new egg-laying spots.

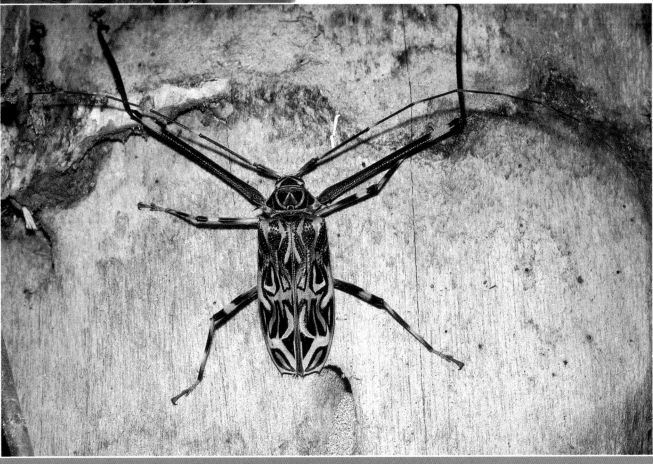

403

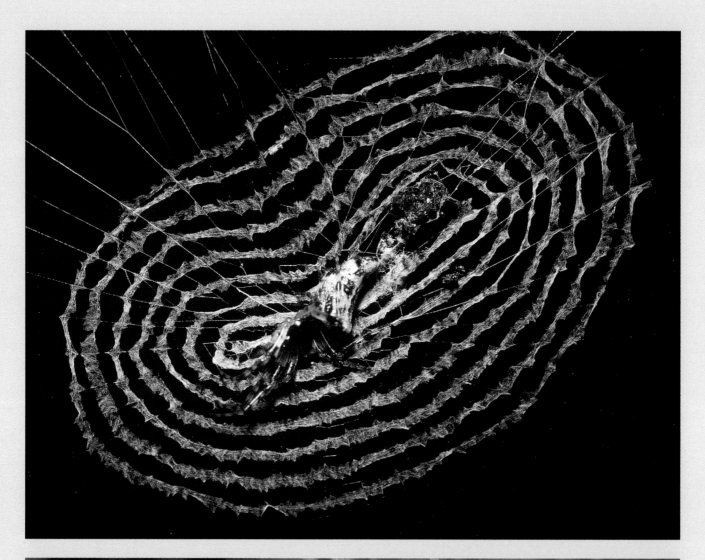

RAINFOREST CAMOUFLAGE

Left: The very widespread decoy spider (*Cyclosa insulana*) spins a spiral stabilimentum of shining white silk in the centre of its web. It then sits near the centre, alongside a few carefully sited bits of debris from former prey, which the spider itself strongly resembles. Only the experienced eye would pick out the spider, even though it is sitting in full view.

Below Left: The photographer initially took this *Alcidodes* weevil in a Kenyan rainforest to be just a small piece of broken-off twig, of which there are millions of pieces lying around on the ground-floor vegetation, especially after heavy rains have swept the canopy clean of anything remotely loose. By having a roughened finish, the orange rear end to the weevil's body mimics the pale jagged end where the stick was broken off.

Right: Many crab spiders sit on matching backgrounds. In this case, a skipper butterfly has failed to spot the *Misumenops* crab spider perched on white flowers on the rainforest edge in Trinidad.

Below: The 12-spined weevil (*Rhigus horridus*) normally sits well above the ground on a leaf, where its hard and lumpy body makes it a fairly unappetising prospect, even in the unlikely event that it is recognised as a living creature (and potential meal) in the first place. Like most of its relatives, any nearby disturbance causes a quick reaction—the weevil dives off its leaf and drops like a stone. Once on the ground, it is virtually impossible to pick out against the pale dead leaves on the rainforest floor. Brazil.

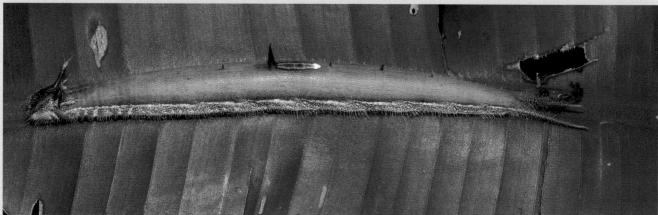

Top: This *Thomisus* crab spider is so invisible on a yellow flower that it is hardly surprising that it easily caught a butterfly that came to feed.

Above: The huge caterpillar of the cocoa mort-bleu, (*Caligo teucer insulanus*), an enormous owl butterfly from Trinidad, spends the day neatly aligned with the sunken midrib of the large *Heliconia* leaf on which it feeds. By disposing itself so carefully, it becomes far less conspicuous than it would be up on the convex outer sections of the leaf.

Above Right: Defence in depth. The defensive ploy adopted by this *Eutelia* moth caterpillar (Noctuidae) in Kenya operates on a dual principle. Firstly, by covering itself completely in a dry crust of own droppings, it ends up

not looking much like a caterpillar. Secondly, even if its cover is blown, it won't present a very appetising prospect for most predators.

Right: These *Noroma nigrolunata* moths (Lymantriidae) mating in full view in day-time on the female's newly-vacated pupal case in a Ugandan rainforest were first mistaken for a fallen white feather—a common enough sight. The photographer walked back and forth past them several times before finally deciding to take a closer look, and that only because of a shortage of other subjects. It is not rare for male moths to seek out females emerging from their pupa, thereby ensuring the virginal status that is of such vital interest to many male 'bugs', especially where females only mate but once during their lifetime.

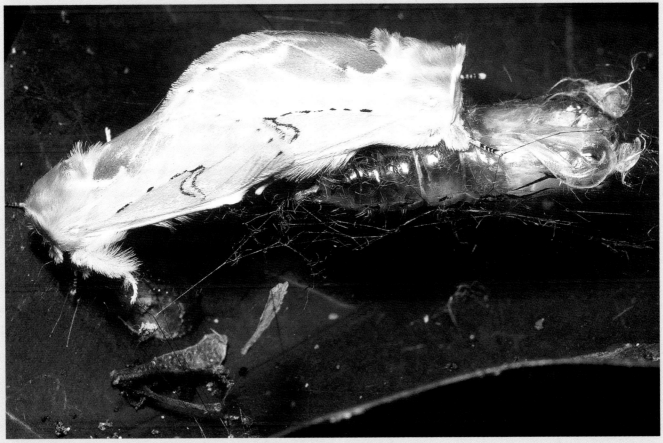

THE OTHER EXTREME— WARNING COLOURATION

Right: The caterpillar of *Coeliades keithloa*, a skipper butterfly from Kenya, exhibits a very common warning pattern of black and orange bands, seen in chemically protected 'bugs' around the world. The common adoption of such a boldly proclaimed uniform has great advantages for its wearers, because it saves predators the task of having to learn a confusing variety of different warning patterns, a key element in the development of mimicry.

Inset Right: Warning colouration is often more effective when applied en masse, as practised by these moth caterpillars eating a poisonous *Solanum* leaf in Mexico. However, there is also another good reason for staying together. These caterpillars will all be from the same egg-batch, and so are therefore brothers and sisters. As an inexperienced and particularly hungry predator may be tempted to risk taking a sample, one member of the group may have to die. However, its death is not entirely in vain, as the unpleasant experience of its going will have persuaded the predator that it is not a good idea to touch any more of the group. It is better to sacrifice your life in the future interests of your kith and kin, rather than to die alone and in vain.

Below: Insects that feed on passion flower vines absorb a variety of unpleasant chemicals, giving them an effective form of chemical protection against most enemies, something that is normally advertised by warning colours. This *Heliconius sara* butterfly caterpillar from South America also has a secondary defensive armament of long spines.

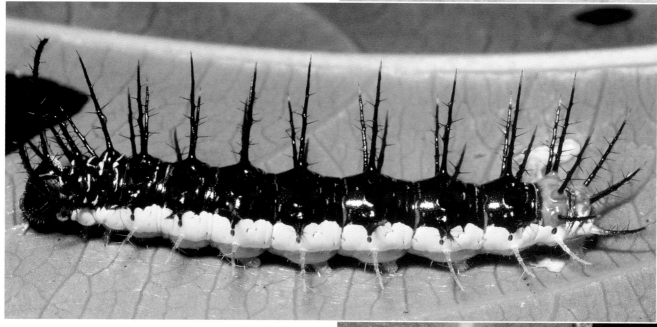

Left: The caterpillar of the frangipani hawk moth (*Pseudosphinx tetrio*) is a large spectacular beast that feeds singly but may congregate to startling effect on the trunk of its food plant, which may be stripped bare by its depredations. Peru.

Below: A twin pair of stink glands clearly visible in the middle of the back give a clue as to why these *Lyramorpha* bug nymphs are clustered together in such a flamboyant fashion on a leaf in an Australian rainforest. The repellent odour given off by goading this gorgeous troupe into retaliating is quite nauseating.

Bottom: In many insects, such as the large *Eutropidacris cristata* grasshoppers from South America, the nymphs, with their limited mobility, are warningly coloured but the adults, which can fly away to escape from trouble, are cryptic. Black and yellow stripes is another very common warning pattern, seen on everything from caterpillars and flatworms to wasps and spiders. Costa Rica.

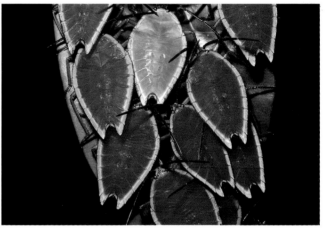

Above: The adults of the leaf-footed bug *Spartocera fusca* from Mexico are solitary and quite drably coloured, but the nymphs live in large warningly coloured aggregations.

Right: Life-saving measures start early in most 'bugs'. These tiny *Edessa* stink bug nymphs from Trinidad are already carrying their red warning uniforms, even though they are newly hatched and still clustered around their recently vacated egg-shells. The adults are large, impressive beasts, with striped warningly coloured under-sides—but they are not red. The first meal for the newly-emerged nymphs will have been their old egg-shells, from which they take up special bacteria that are essential for the proper digestion of their plant food. The bacteria are smeared onto the eggs by the female as she lays each one, and are derived from special storage organs in the female's body.

Previous Page: Most members of the 'cottonstainer' bug family Pyrrhocoridae are warningly coloured, often scarlet like this *Dindymus* species feeding on a small caterpillar in Sumatran rainforest. Many 'cottonstainer' species form dense aggregations, both as nymphs and adults.

Left: Like many warningly coloured moths, *Gymnelia ethodaea* (Arctiidae) from Mexico is active in daylight, when its visual 'keep off' message can best be seen and acknowledged. It belongs to the subfamily Ctenuchinae, most of which are day-flying chemically protected species, often resembling wasps or ichneumons.

Below Left: Another large genus of warningly coloured geometrid moths is *Dysphania*. This is *Dysphania contraria* from Sulawesi, resting on the rainforest floor having probably recently emerged from its pupa.

Right: Sometimes warning colours are kept under wraps until a situation develops when sudden drastic action is needed. This *Dirphia avia* moth from Trinidad is quite inconspicuous when at rest with closed wings. If touched, it sits tight and throws its wings forward to reveal a striking red and black abdomen. In some species of *Dirphia* the abomen is banded with black and white, another common warning combination.

Below Right: Many rainforest larvae, such as this arctiid caterpillar from Trinidad, combine warning colours with a defensive stockade of stinging spines.

Above: The African moth *Aletis erici* is not only warningly coloured in its own right, it is also a member of a large mimicry ring. Most of the other members are butterflies, and the linchpin for the ring, the core model on which the colour and pattern of all the others are based is probably the widespread and very common African monarch butterfly (*Danaus chrysippus*), also called the plain tiger.

Right: In Africa there is black and white mimicry ring centred on various unpalatable *Amauris* butterflies, such as the novice *Amauris ochlea*. The ring includes *Graphium philione*, a palatable Batesian mimic (see glossary), which unlike most members of the swallowtail family (Papilonidae) lacks tails, so as to more closely match the tail less *Amauris* models.

ARMOUR AS DEFENCE

Some rainforest insects are perfectly good to eat and are relatively clumsy and slow-moving, so cannot easily run away from danger. Many species therefore combine a strategy of looking as inconspicuous as possible, combined with heavy armour to act as protection if they are discovered. Many warningly coloured 'bugs' are also armoured, giving them the vital ability to withstand a brief speculative attack by an inexperienced enemy without suffering a fatal level of damage.

Top: This large *Phoberodema* katydid from Australia is well camouflaged when at rest on a tree trunk or branch. Its thorax is bristling with a defensive stockade of thick, sharp spines. If touched it will stick its very spiny legs out in all directions and try to rake the back legs down the face or nose of an aggressor.

Above: *Cosmoderus erinaceus* is an extravagantly armoured katydid from the rainforests of Uganda. It spends the day hidden between two leaves, but if cornered, it must rely on its spiny armour, as it is wingless and cannot escape by flying.

Right: *Pseudorhynchus pungens* is a large katydid from Uganda. If picked up it bites fiercely and powerfully, and would be difficult to swallow because of the sharp and rigid horn projecting upwards from the head.

EGG-LAYING AND PARENTING

Below: Many click beetles (Elateridae) lay eggs in diseased or fallen trees. The large, handsome *Semiotus insignis* from Costa Rica is warningly coloured, and this female spent more than an hour running up and down along a fallen tree in the shady forest interior, stopping now and then to probe into the bark with her ovipositor, hoping to find the best location to lay her eggs.

Bottom: The process of decay in fallen trees is greatly accelerated by fungi whose mycelial strands permeate the interior of the wood. When the rains arrive, the log suddenly sprouts a forest of fungal fruiting bodies. The female of the fungus beetle *Pselephacus giganteus* has to find the fruiting bodies when they are mere buds, providing fresh tender food for her

brood of tiny wriggling babies. Here the female is gathering the babies together before shepherding them across to a new source of food. Under their mother's expert care the larvae feed continuously and grow at an amazing rate, which is just as well as the swiftly expanding fungi only last for a few days before decaying and disintegrating. Trinidad.

Right: When a rainforest tree topples to the ground with an earth-shaking crash, the space it occupied is soon cluttered with a tangle of vines, which attract ovi-positing butterflies such as this king cracker (*Hamadryas amphinome*) female in Trinidad. The males produce a loud cracking sound from their wings in flight, thought to be connected with defence of territory.

Above: In the tortoise beetle *Acromis sparsa* from South America the female lays a string of eggs beneath the leaf of a vine and then stands guard over them until they hatch. As her babies grow she remains with them, perching herself on top of the compact group that they form when not feeding. She will leave her perch in order to chase away an intruding ant or assassin bug and is fearless in defence of her brood, even staying on to guard the cluster of pupae which are eventually formed near the base of the food plant.

Left: A number of assassin bugs guard their eggs. This female *Pisilus tipuliformis rufipes* female in Uganda is on close alert as her babies hatch from a batch of eggs that she has been guarding for nearly two weeks. Unlike the tortoise and fungus beetles, she deserts her young soon after they have safely emerged.

Right: Under cover of darkness in a Brazilian rainforest a female *Deinopis* net-casting spider carefully adds a swaddling of silk to her egg-sac, suspended from a long silken line above the rainforest floor. Later she will add a few scraps of dead leaf as camouflage just above the egg-sac, which soon turns brown, making the finished article very hard to spot in the gloom of the rainforest understorey.

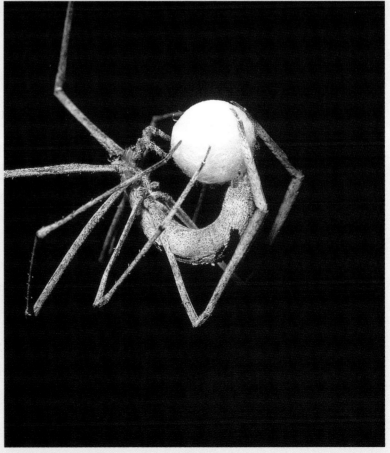

THE RAINFOREST MATING GAME

The rainforest is a very large, complex and crowded environment in which millions of 'bugs' are simultaneously trying to find a mate of their own kind. In such a chaotic situation it is vital that each sex should announce its presence in a clear and unambiguous way, thereby speeding up any eventual rendezvous and ensuring that only a mate of the correct species is attracted. Even when a male and female have met for the first time, mating may have to wait until some kind of formal and ritualised courtship has established the credentials of the suitor, usually the male. Here are a few of the variations.

Above: *Nyssodesmus python* is a large, warningly coloured flat-backed millipede that makes its way around the rainforest floor feeding on dead leaves and so playing a role in the vital process of recycling the rainforest nutrients. During courtship the male straddles the female and nibbles her face, trying to persuade her to accept him, usually with little success. It is not rare to see two males simultaneously engaged in trying to coax the same female to make herself available, as seen here in lowland rainforest in Costa Rica.

Top: The tiny male of the giant wood spider (*Nephila maculata*) also uses silk, which he lays down in a thin and almost invisible skein across the back of the huge female. She usually ignores his excursions to and fro across her bulky back, but may become sufficiently irritated to flick the male off with her long legs, rather like ridding herself of an annoying fly. The reason for the silk-laying process is unknown, especially as mating often takes place without it, mainly when the female has her mind on other things, such as feeding on a juicy fly. Sulawesi.

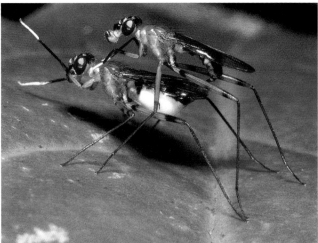

Top: Male stilt-legged flies (Micropezidae), such as this *Ptilosphen insignis* from Trinidad, generally employ their white front legs in a semaphoring courtship. In some species the female may turn her head back and 'kiss' the mate sitting on her back, during which he transfers part of his liquid stomach-contents to her as a 'wedding gift'.

Above: Rivalry often breaks out in praying mantises. Probably responding to the summons of 'come and get me' pheromones released by the female, a male *Acontista* mantis in Trinidad has dropped in, only to find that some rival made his entrance first and has claimed the female. As sexually responsive females are in short supply, the new arrival cannot merely 'shrug his shoulders' and accept the situation, he must try and retrieve the situation by forcing his rival to dismount. The only way to do this is either to pull or push him bodily off the female, and this is the ploy that is currently being tried in the illustration. Unfortunately the mating pair enjoy the advantage of a strong genital tie, making it highly unlikely that they can be forcibly uncoupled. For the female, gaining a new mate who has proved himself in battle against her current consort would be an advantage, but in this instance the aggressor eventually gave up the hopeless task and flew off.

Left: In the African lynx spider *Oxyopes schenkeli* a brief initial bout of stroking by the male persuades the female to dive off a leaf on her drag-line. The males follows her down, and then twirls her round and round in mid-air, wrapping her in a bridal veil of silk before mating takes place.

Right: Female beetles often spend very long periods when they are unwilling to accept a mate. In such difficult circumstances a male will often try and guard the female against any rivals who may locate her, basing this on the hope that if he stays around long enough he might eventually get lucky. In response to the imminent intrusion of a competitor moving in from the right, this male *Neptunides polychromus* chafer (left) is spreading his front legs over a female's rear end, ready to repel all-comers from this vital region. Uganda.

Below: Male tiger beetles spend long periods with their large jaws clamped around a special coupling-groove on the female's body. This strong tie reduces the male's chances of being displaced by a competitor during the long guarding period between mating and the moment when the female finally lays her eggs. This is *Cicindela aurulenta* from Borneo.

Bottom: In many butterflies the courting male flutters around the female, showering her with special scent-laden scales. Once mated, they sit in a back-to-back position, although most species sit with the wings closed, unlike these *Neptidopsis ophiona* from Kenya.

RAINFOREST ANTS

Ants abound in the rainforest, from three centimetre-long (one inch-long) monsters with a sting to match their size, to tiny varieties thousands of times smaller. Some ants are scavengers while others are fearsome killers, and none more so than the notorious *Eciton* army ants, the South American equivalent of the African driver ants. Army ants have similar habits, constructing only temporary bivouacs whose outer walls are formed from a tangled mass of ants clinging together, often in the sheltered hollow of a tree-base. These nests send out raiding swarms, up to 700,000 strong, which saturate the area and kill anything that gets in the way. The returning columns of booty-laden workers are able to hurry back to the nest with relative ease as any awkward gaps in the forest floor are spanned by bridges of living workers. These cling resolutely in place as thousands of their nest-mates rush across at full speed, often burdened with prey of such magnitude that several workers are needed to carry it. Like many termites the ants are blind, and carry out all this complex labour by following scent-trails laid out by scouts.

Whereas army ants can exert a significant effect locally on the animal life of the South American rainforests, the leaf-cutting ants can exert a similarly large effect on the vegetation, as they are major predators of leaves and even giant trees can suffer heavily. It is common to see a broad column of workers trotting jerkily down a tree-trunk and heading out across the forest floor, making for their huge subterranean nest. Each hurrying worker carries an irregularly-shaped section of leaf which it has snipped away with its jaws. The ants do not eat the leaves, but use them as compost for

Right: *Eciton burchelli* army ants hurry across a bridge made of their fellow workers' bodies. Trinidad.

Below Right: Several *Eciton burchelli* army ants co-operate to carry a large centipede back to the nest. Trinidad.

Below: This *Ectatomma tuberculatom* ant is towing a large cockroach back to the nest in Trinidad.

Below: A large column of *Atta sexdens* leaf-cutter ants crosses the rainforest floor in Brazil.

Bottom: *Atta cephalotes* leaf-cutter ants in Costa Rica.

Right: Leaf-cutter ant soldiers have large heads and jaws.

Below Right: A trio of *Dolichoderus atellaboides* ants feed on extra-floral nectaries near the leaf-bases of an *Inga* tree in Brazil.

the cultivation of the special fungus that is their only food and that is not found outside the fungus gardens in their nests. The soldiers are impressive insects, with large heads and formidable jaws, and the leaf-cutting ants are among the few creatures virtually immune to attack by the army ant hordes.

Not all trees have such a loss-making relationship with ants. Many of them adopt ants as guardians by providing them with food.

Weaver ants merely make temporary use of the living leaves as nests, tacking them together using the silk from a pupa held in a worker's jaws. Ants also affect plants by guarding their enemies, such as sap-sucking treehoppers or certain butterfly caterpillars. These have glandular secretions that stimulate such a level of craving in the ants that they will form a living coat on the caterpillar's body, ready to defend it to the death if necessary.

LIFE ON A FALLEN TREE IN A KENYAN RAINFOREST

A fallen tree is a Mecca for a host of insects. As light floods into the previously gloomy forest floor, the tree itself begins the slow process of decay, and at this early stage it will be attractive to a wide range of wood-feeding insects. The first to arrive are usually the beetles. Some of these are brightly coloured, such as the variable longhorn (*Sternotomis variabilis*), a common species. The females bite holes in the bark and then turn around to lay eggs in the slits thus produced. They are often accompanied by males, who tag-along behind in a half-mount position; not actually mating, yet ready to jump off and drive away any intruding males. Mating takes place just before the female lays an egg, when her mate can be absolutely sure that he will be the father. The strange daddy-longlegs weevils have similar habits, but the male, who is huge compared with the female, trots along behind her and 'cages' her beneath his gangly legs.

As the beetle larvae get to work on the timber a new set of opportunities arises on the fallen tree. A flow of sticky sap may

Top: A *Calais* species click beetle on a fallen tree.

Above: Green-veined charaxes butterfly (*Charaxes candiope*) feeding on fermenting sap. Kenya.

Above Right: This large *Sipalinus squalidus* weevil looks like a gnarled lump on the bark.

Right: A variable longhorn male (*Sternotomis varabilis*) mate-guarding a female about to lay an egg.

Above: A giant male daddy-longlegs weevil *Mecopus torquis* cages the tiny female beneath his long legs and projecting rostrum.

Right: The same tree also attracted a delicate-looking silver-striped charaxes (*Charaxes lasti*).

erupt from a beetle gallery, and this resinous material can be of great interest to tiny *Trigona* stingless bees, which will gather it on their back legs and use it for nesting material. If the sap starts to ferment it will attract beetles, flies and butterflies, some of which get so drunk that they can scarcely fly when touched, and can simply be picked up off the tree.

WASPS' NESTS IN SOUTH AMERICAN RAINFORESTS

Above: Wasps' nests come in a wide variety of architectural styles and are founded in different ways. Some are initiated by a single queen, later to be joined by a retinue of subservient helpers. Others are established by mass-swarming, as in the case of *Polybia occidentalis,* and in this type of nest there is also a division of labour. Some workers just gather paper-pulp, scraping fine wood-shavings from trees with their jaws. Others are water-carriers, who supply the pulp-gatherers with the liquid needed for mixing up the pulp. Finally there are builders, who receive the pulp supplies from the incoming gatherers and perform the skilled work of adding it rapidly to the expanding nest. The final structure has a complex series of internal combs, protected by an outer envelope which usually has a row of 'drip-tips' attached to the the underside.

Left: The nest of *Stelopolybia palipes* is an inverted funnel on the underside of a leaf, which acts as an umbrella, keeping the nest dry.

Above: Parasol wasps are unusual in being exclusively nocturnal. They spend the day neatly arranged on the surface of their nest, which has open cells as in the *Polistes* wasp discussed in the desert chapter. This is *Apoica pallens*, which has quite a severe sting. The nests of some species of *Apoica* can reach a diameter of over 60 centimetres (two feet).

Left: Like *Polistes*, *Mischocyttarus alfkenii* builds an open nest in which the larvae are clearly visible (one at the top-right is poking its head right out of its cell). The capped cells visible contain pupae, while one of the workers, near the bottom, is offering a larva the chewed remains of a caterpillar. In return the larva will regurgitate a droplet of saliva for the adult, which cannot eat solid food.

Right: In *Mischocyttarus vaqueroi* the nest is unusual in being a long twig-like structure consisting of a simple string of single cells placed end-on-end. The nests are often suspended from beneath the roofs of huts built in the rainforest.

Below: *Charterginus fulvus* builds a beautiful star-like and very delicate paper nest beneath a large leaf. There is just a single entrance, visible at top-left, with a wasp just entering.

Right: A number of wasps, including *Polybia occidentalis*, store nectar in their nests, but in *Brachygastra mellifica* large amounts of honey are stored in a very bee-like behaviour pattern.

Below: The mud-dauber *Sceliphron fistularum* is not a social wasp, but builds its nest as a solo enterprise. This female is laying down a new cell on top of one that has just been completed and closed. She works swiftly, expertly dribbling her pellet of soft mud along the work surface with her jaws, all the while buzzing her wings which vibrates the malleable material and facilitates its smooth flow into the correct place. Each cell is built as a cylinder, starting at the back and finishing at the front, and will be filled with a series of paralysed spiders before finally being closed with mud.

SO MANY WAYS TO BE A GREEN LEAF

The prevailing colour in rainforests throughout the year is green. Unlike in deciduous forests, the leaves of the rainforest trees and shrubs are mostly very long-lived and may last for years. This leads to a gradual change in the leaf's appearance, from a fresh green youngster to tired old-timer, disfigured by blemishes and encrusted with mosses and lichens. There are 'bugs' that faithfully copy every aspect of those years of gradual change, so much so that they can be a leaf and sit where they like, not just on a leafy background.

Below: *Pycnopalpa cordata* is a widespread South American katydid that mimics a much smaller leaf that is beginning to suffer from terminal decline, with symptoms of fungal attack and a 'blotching' caused by a moth.

Bottom: *Sasima truncata* is a large katydid from New Guinea. Apart from its very credible leaf-mimicry, it has a couple of other defensive strategies. The top of the thorax is heavily armoured and ringed by spines and if touched the katydid instantly sticks its back legs vertically up in the air. This might seem a suicidal thing to do, but the legs are bright yellow and red, so probably serve as a warning that their owner, although relying on leaf-mimicry for its primary defence, is actually chemically protected.

Left: This large *Paracycloptera* katydid from Costa Rica occurs in a number of colour forms, each mimicking a leaf in a different stage of decline. In this form the 'leaf' is speckled with pale spots resulting from 'insect' attack and has a 'hole' where something has nibbled through it.

Top and Above: In most rainforest katydids the adults and nymphs employ different defensive strategies. The nymphs are often speckled with silvery-blue spots and sit with their legs stretched out backwards while their head is positioned just above the leaf-tip. They are surprisingly difficult to spot in this position, and could possibly be mimicking the rain-speckled leaves that are such a normal feature of the rainforest. It can be difficult to associate such a nymph correctly with the eventual adult, but in this case it seems to be a *Debrona* species (top), which is a leaf-mimic in the adult stage, and also adopts a similar posture.

EVEN MORE WAYS TO MIMIC A DEAD LEAF

Dead leaves abound in rainforests, but not in the same way is in a deciduous forest. In the latter the mass leaf-fall in autumn leads to the formation of a permanent carpet of dead leaves. By contrast, rainforest leaves mainly fall in dribs and drabs throughout the year. Many of them never even reach the ground, as they fall upon the dense layer of evergreen vegetation in the forest understorey, and this is where most dead-leaf mimics live. Unfortunately, staged photographs have perpetuated the myth that dead-leaf mimics not only live among leaves on the forest floor, but even select leaves that are a precise match for themselves. In the interests of scientific veracity, the 'bugs' illustrated in this section are on backgrounds chosen by themselves rather than by the photographer.

Above Left: Being flattened, fast-running detritus-feeders, many cockroaches are more at home on the forest floor than anywhere else, as this provides them with plenty of food to be scavenged during their nocturnal forays. Their main enemies are ants, especially army or driver ants, which are not fooled by the cockroach's resemblance to a dead leaf. This *Rhabdoblatta* species is from Kenya.

Left: *Colpolopha burmeisteri* from South America is one of only a very small number of grasshoppers that live on the rainforest floor. The nymphs are actually better camouflaged than the adult pictured here, whose wings are something of a give-away.

Top: A dead-leaf personified, this *Chorotypus* monkeyhopper from Malaysia is even flattened like a leaf, having a wafer-thin body in which the internal organs must be remarkably crowded. Note how it is up on low vegetation, never among dead leaves on the forest floor. This species can also be green, mimicking a living leaf, or half-and-half, mimicking a leaf on the wane.

Above: The wingless female of *Acanthops falcata*—a small, flightless South American mantis—looks like a curled, shrivelled leaf. If under attack she can resort to a fall-back device and raises her wing-cases to reveal a shiny red and black top to her abdomen, designed (probably under false-pretences) to function as a warning signal. The male is fully winged and resembles a flatter, less shrivelled leaf. Neither sex lives on the forest floor, although they are often portrayed as such.

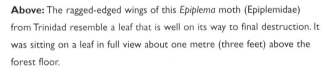

Above: The ragged-edged wings of this *Epiplema* moth (Epiplemidae) from Trinidad resemble a leaf that is well on its way to final destruction. It was sitting on a leaf in full view about one metre (three feet) above the forest floor.

Left: *Phyllocrania illudens* from Africa and Madagascar is one of the most convincing of many kinds of dead-leaf mantids from around the tropical world. The nymph is a fantastically credible mimic of a shrivelled leaf. Both adult and nymph normally hang head-downards, like a leaf which has died but not fallen, waiting for prey to come close. In this instance the adult pictured was moving its place of ambush, thereby betraying its presence to the photographer. In dry forest types this species is a pale whitish-brown, matching the sun-dried leaves typical of such areas.

Left: *Nyceryx tacita* from Peru is one of a small number of hawkmoths that are reasonable mimics of dead leaves, but not really good enough to escape detection when sitting in the open on a non-matching background. The moths are therefore adept at searching out genuine dead leaves on which to spend the day.

Right: Many dead leaves curl and are caught by plant stems as they fall. By clasping a stem between its wings, leaving its plump body hanging down below, this *Mimallo amilia* moth (Mimallonidae) in Trinidad resembles such a leaf, and holds its pose throughout the day, even during a tropical deluge.

Far Right: Most dead-leaf butterflies make no attempt to select a matching background, but merely exploit the freedom given by their convincing mimicry to perch wherever they want. Most species hang-upside down, as in this *Salamis anteva* from Madagascar, in such a way that the pointed tips to the hindwings mimic the stalk attaching the 'leaf' to the stem.

Below Right: The number of dead-leaf mimics among katydids is legion. This Typophyllum from South America can occur in a huge variety of forms, mimicking everything from fresh green leaves, through yellowing ones in rapid decline to the thoroughly dead example seen here. The daylight hours are spent hanging beneath any leaves that happen to be handy (not sitting upright among precisely-matching leaves, as often falsely depicted). At night the risk of being seen by sharp-eyed enemies such as birds is largely over, and these katydids safely emerge and sit in on the upper surface of a leaf, where they are relatively easy to find using a flashlight.

Below: Some moths have a more sophisticated pose. By clinging to a fallen twig sticking up vertically from the forest floor, the geometrid Hyposidra talaca from Australia resembles a single dead leaf that has failed to become detached as the twig fell, a fairly common occurrence.

445

WHEN IS A WASP NOT A WASP?

Most animals quickly learn two important facts about wasps. Firstly, they have an unpleasant sting and secondly, not getting stung again is going to be easy because wasps have an easily recognised combination of shape, pattern and style of moving so they can be easily avoided. The stage is therefore set for a whole troupe of harmless and not-so-harmless 'bugs' to impersonate wasps and earn themselves the same level of immunity to attack.

South America has the greatest range of wasp-mimics, of which the most common is the 'yellow' mimicry ring broadly based on numerous smallish wasps exemplified by *Polybia catillifex*. The most amazing member of this ring is probably *Lissocarta vespifromis*, an extremely unusual leaf hopper bug in which the transparent wings are held up wasp-like above the body, while the abdomen has a wasp-like shape and waist. Just as a reminder of the sweeping evolutionary changes this species has made in order to perfect its copycat image compare it with the more typical Peruvian specimen illustrated bottom right, with its colourful wings held tent-like close above the body.

Another superb member of the 'yellow' mimicry ring is a remarkable *Sphodrolestes* assassin bug from the Brazilian rainforests. This will be a Müllerian mimic, as it has a formidable 'bite' which is far more painful than many wasp stings. Most *Climaciella* mantispids are also wasp-mimics and some species occur in a wide variety of forms, each mimicking a different species of wasp, such as the dark-bodied *Stelopolybia pallipes*. This common wasp forms one of several similar models for the 'dusky' mimicry ring, of which one

Right: *Wissocanta vespifarnis* 'yellow' form.

Below Right: A more 'normal' kind of red hopper from Peru.

Below: *Polybia catillifex* wasps on their nest.

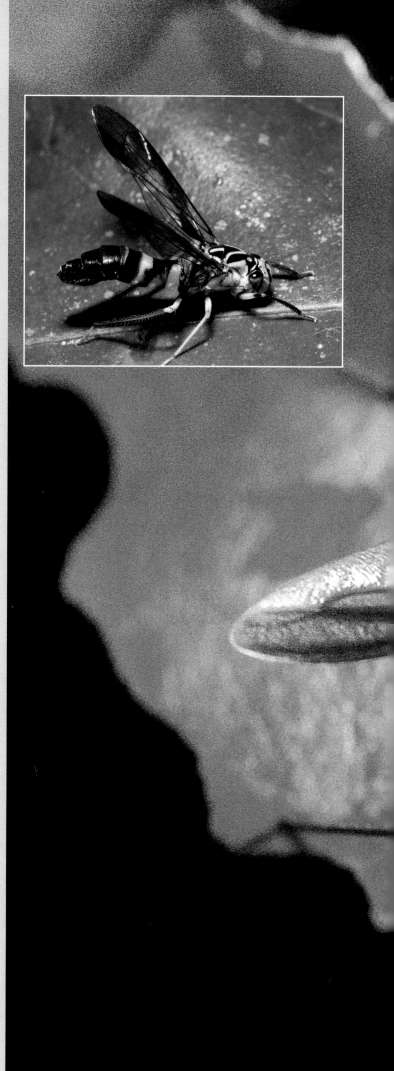

Above: *Climaciella nantispid* in Brazil.

Inset Above Right: *Lissocarta vespifromis* 'dusky' form.

Right: A *Sphodrelesles* assassin bug from Brazil.

member is, yet again, the versatile Lissocarta vespifromis. 'Yellow' and 'dusky' forms of this incredible bug often sit side-by-side on the same leaf. Several small moths are also part of the 'dusky' complex, mostly day-flying arctiids in the subfamily Ctenuchinae.

The above species all mimic social wasps, but the rainforests also abound in many large and formidable solitary wasps, especially large spider-hunters such as *Pepsis* and allied geera. These are mimicked by a several kinds of assassin bugs, as well as by some truly mind-blowing katydids, such as *Scaphura*. Several species have been described, but in reality there is probably only one, which occurs in a plethora of forms, each mimicking a different species of wasp and often occurring together. When at rest with its wings folded *Scaphura* looks fairly wasp-like, but if alarmed it launches into a dramatic and highly convincing act. Flicking its wings convulsively up above its back while curling its abdomen downwards and vibrating

Top: *Monogonogastra sp.* traconid wasp.

Above: *Hiranetis braconiformis* assassin bug sticking out its back leg to mimic the braconid's ovipostor. Peru.

Above Left: Arctiid moth mimicking a wasp. Peru.

Left: *Scaphara* katydid in full display.

its antennae, it sets off in a jerky and spasmodic way over the vegetation, the most perfect imitation imaginable of a large spider-hunting wasp on the quest for a victim. Amazing.

Another piece of incredible behaviour is exhibited by another assassin bug, *Hiranetis braconiformis*. It models itself on various common black and orange braconid wasps, such as *Monogonogastra*, and occurs in different forms mimicking different species. Most braconids active in the forest are females searching for a host, and these have a short ovipositor projecting like a little spike from the rear end. The bug's rear end is innocent of such a distinctive projection, but to make up for this shortfall it sticks one hindleg out behind the tip of its abdomen, thereby acquiring an 'instant'

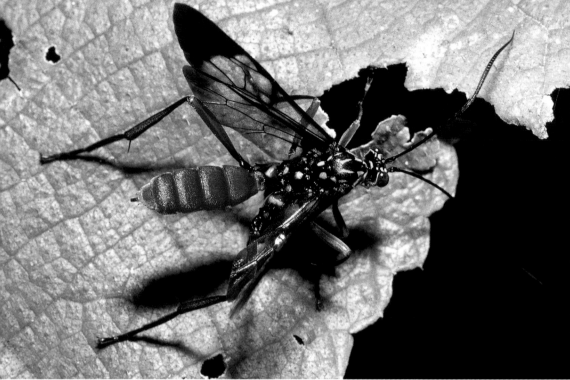

ovipositor. The bug only pulls this trick when closely threatened, when its already excellent mimicry might need just that extra crumb of verisimilitude.

The scarlet and black uniform worn by many South American parasitic wasps is mimicked by a variety of insects, but particularly by many kinds of *Holhymenia* bugs (Coreidae). These feed on passion flower vines, which means that they are going to be distasetful Müllerian mimics. The katydid nymph illustrated right is quite remarkable as it lacks the transparent wings present in a real wasp. To make up for this important deficiency, the top of the nymph's abdomen is decorated with a very credible wing-like pattern, while its habit of moving in a very jerky way, constantly quivering its antennae, lends a powerful dose of authenticity to its performance.

Above: A typical black and red parasitic wasp.

Right: A wasp-mimicking katydid nymph. Peru.

Inset Right: *Holhymenia sp.* assassin bug. Peru.

ARE WE ANTS?

Ants are not an attractive source of food for most predators. Their sting can be unpleasantly painful and long-lasting, made the more unwelcome by often being delivered in some numbers. Ants also appear to have a fairly unappetising flavour and relatively few animals will eat them, despite the fact that they are virtually ubiquitous. Given all this, it is quite obvious that there are major advantages in adopting the same general profile as an ant, thereby gaining the same degree immunity from attack, yet without being able to back it up with any offensive hardware.

Above: Several South American species of treehopper bug manage ant-mimicry quite convincingly, including this *Heteronotus* species from Brazil. Several of these bugs are 'reversed-end' mimics, meaning that the pronotum (the area of the thorax just behind the head) is modified such that its rear end resembles the open jaws of an ant sitting in an alert pose on a leaf.

Below Left: This *Taeniaptera* stilt-legged fly (Micropezidae) carries out its act on vegetation near the forest floor. Its small transparent wings tend to merge imperceptibly into the abdomen, which is highly unusual (for a fly), and an ant-like stalk connects the abdomen to the thorax. Like most good ant-mimics it completes the picture by moving in a restless ant-like way.

Above Right: In Australia the commonest rainforest ant in some areas is the green tree ant (*Oecophylla smaragdina*) which, as its name suggests, is green. It says much for the perfection so regularly achieved by mimetic insects that this *Riptortus* bug nymph is also green. It belongs to the family Alydidae, a widespread family (in temperate zones as well as rainforests) in which the nymphs are almost always very ant-like, and normally closely correspond to the commonest species of ant in their area.

Right: Just to prove how good the *Riptortus* is, here are some real green tree ants, in a defensive stance on a *Narathura* butterfly caterpillar. Like many members of the Lycaenidae, this caterpillar has glands which secrete a sugary liquid of compulsive attraction for ants, hence their willingness to die in its defence. Many lycaenid caterpillars are taken back to the nest by the ants, where they repay their hosts by consuming their brood.

DON'T EAT ME, I'M JUST A BIRD-DROPPING

Birds don't go round looking for their own droppings to eat, so mimicking a dropping is a sensible survival stratagem that has been adopted by a wide range of 'bugs' around the world. Here is a selection from the rainforests.

Below: *Verrucosa meridionalis* is an orb-web spider from Argentina. It is one of several related species that do not sit in the web but rest instead on a nearby leaf, with the legs held in close to the body. This helps to lend credibility to the overall impression of a fairly neat-and-tidy dropping that has landed reasonably intact.

Left: The physiological and behavioural modifications seen in this katydid nymph probably make it the most impressive of all the bird-dropping mimics. It is probably *Pycnopalpa bicordata*, which if true would involve a radical switch to leaf-mimicry in the adult stage. Note how the legs, with their flattened shiny outgrowths, are splayed out flat at the sides in order to copy the way a genuine dropping would splash outwards and scatter as it hits the leaf. Note also how the tip of the abdomen is held bent to one side, thereby destroying the nymph's natural symmetry and more faithfully portraying the random shape of a real dropping.

Top: The young caterpillars of many swallowtail butterflies are among the best bird-dropping mimics. This is the caterpillar of the king page swallow-tail (*Papilio thoas*) from South America.

Above: The hair-fringed legs of this *Euproctis conizona* moth (Lymantriidae) from Kenya imitate the splashed-out liquid contents of the dropping. If its deception should fail, this moth can resort to a back-up defensive ploy. It sits tight and sticks the reddish-haired tip of its abdomen up between its wing-cases, a warning signal that indicates that it is not good to eat.

FOREST TIGERS

Walking through any South American rainforest you soon become aware that many of the butterflies look monotonously similar, with rather narrow wings having yellow, black or orange stripes. In fact dozens of species are involved, in several families, and they all look similar because they are members of the 'tiger-striped' mimicry ring, which includes both Batesian and Müllerian mimics. The most abundant members of the ring in most habitats, and also probably the 'core' models for the whole complex, are various species of ithomiine butterflies (family Nymphalidae). A small sample of other members is illustrated.

Right: *Mechanitis lysimnia* (Nymphalidae: Ithomiinae) is one of the core members of the "tiger-striped' mimicry complex.

Below: *Phyciodes eunice* (Nymphalidae) is a Batesian member of the 'tiger-striped' mimicry ring.

Left: In the 'tiger-striped' mimicry ring, as in other rings in both South America and Africa, the undersides of the wings are also involved. This is a distasteful 'model', *Tithoria harmonia* (Nymphalidae: Ithomiinae).

Top: The day-flying moth *Dysschema irene* (Arctiidae) is a Müllerian member of the ring.

Above: The tiger pierid *Dismorphia amphione* is part of the 'tiger-striped' ring, which leads to a narrow wing profile quite unlike most members of its family Pieridae.

HEADS OR TAILS?

The most vulnerable part of any 'bug' is its head, and this is where most predators (especially birds) will aim a first blow. If the predator's attention can be redirected towards some other less delicate and vital part of the body, it could save a life. Many 'bugs' therefore sport a duplicate 'head' aimed at misdirecting an enemy's initial attack and buying precious time for a rapid escape.

Below: This *Lirimiris* moth caterpillar (Notodontidae) from Costa Rica responds to disturbance by tucking its real head in beside its body and expanding a bulbous false-head at its rear end. Its colours seem to fall into the warning category, so the caterpillar's strategy is probably of a delaying nature only, aimed at keeping its head in place while giving the enemy a taste of something nasty from the rear end.

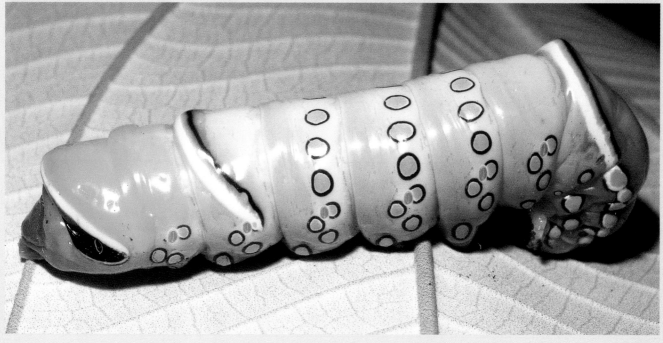

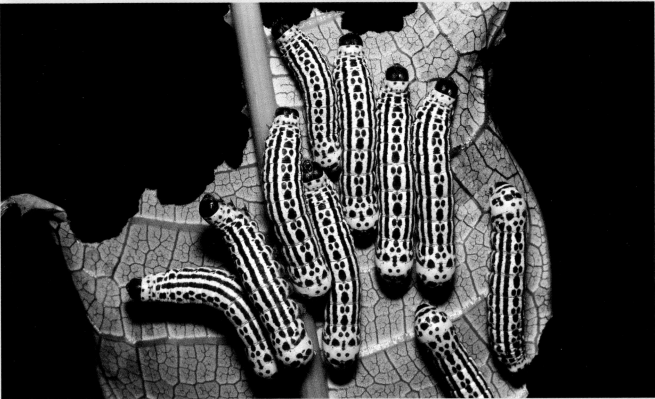

Left: This spectacular *Naprepa* moth caterpillar (Notodontidae) in Costa Rica adopts a similar strategy but this time it tucks its head in beneath its body, leaving two eye-like markings at the rear end to distract the enemy's atention. This caterpillar too is warningly coloured, so once again this is probably just a life-saving delaying exercise.

Top: When this hairy moth caterpillar (Noctuidae) in Sumatra is touched it curls up, hides its head beneath its body and sticks its rear end upwards towards the adversary. This reveals two white, eye-like markings on a black background, very like a head with large staring eyes.

Above: When confronted with this group of warningly coloured caterpillars in a Malaysian forest, few people would guess correctly which end is which. In fact on the upper eight caterpillars the heads point upwards, while in the bottom two they point downwards.

Above: Many adult butterflies have eye-like markings on the wings, which are not going to suffer any terminal damage if a bird takes out a sizeable piece when aiming a mistaken peck at them. In the South American *Marpesia crethon* and its relatives the 'false head' consists of two reddish eye-like markings on the uppersides of the hindwings, tucked in between the 'tails'.

Left: In the common brown ringlet butterfly (*Hypocysta metirius*) from Australia, the combination of white-pupilled eyespots and orange blotching on the hindwings looks like a tiny face peeping out.

Below: In adult butterflies the best-known examples of false-head mimicry occur in many lycaenids and riodinids. Two or more slender tails on the hindwings resembles antennae, below which are one or more dark-pupilled eye-like markings. To add verisimilitude the wings are constantly shuffled up and down, making the 'antennae' move in a lifelike way. This exponent of the art of deception is the six-tailed brushfoot (*Charis chrysus*), a riodinid from Trinidad.

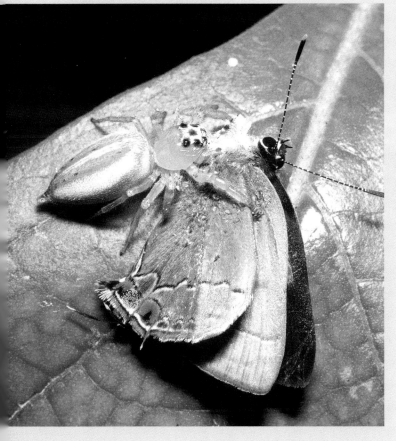

Above: What looks like a perky little cricket's face peering out of a leaf-roll is actually the rear end of the South American orb-web spider *Alpaida truncata*. If its relatively tough hindquarters receive a sudden peck, the spider dashes off to safety in the opposite direction, much to the surprise of its nonplussed attacker.

Left: You win some, you lose some. Certain predators do not target the head, so are not fooled by false-head mimicry. This jumping spider in Peru has caught a lycaenid butterfly, despite its possession of a 'false head' on the hindwings.

WHAT BIG EYES YOU HAVE

'Bugs' don't just try to pretend that their head is in the wrong place—they also try to persuade a potential enemy that they are really just one great big head, with huge, staring, and very threatening eyes. They work this apparent miracle through an act of instant transformation, changing in a flash from harmless 'bug' to a possibly harmful threat. This is mainly a strategy of last-resort, employed in desperation when the 'bug' has already been grabbed or severely handled. It is based on the fact that many common enemies are themselves quite small, and have many enemies of their own, some of which have rather large eyes. Birds especially are nervous, easily startled creatures, virtually guaranteed to be alarmed by the sudden and totally unexpected appearance of a large 'face' staring at them from close range.

Right and Below: The South American lantern fly *Cathedra serrata* is well camouflaged when at rest on a tree trunk. When touched it suddenly opens its wings to reveal a pair of glaring 'eyes'.

A WALK THROUGH A RAINFOREST

Standing in the back of an open pick-up we bump and bang our way along a terrible dirt-road in South America until we arrive at the entrance to a rainforest national park. We pay our small entrance fee at the kiosk and set off down a broad track that runs into the forest and enters a completely different world. The track is muddy, and we have to tread carefully to avoid crushing the hundreds of butterflies and moths that are drinking on the damp ground. The vegetation along the path is about waist-height, and is well-   illuminated because of the width of the track, so there are going to be plenty of 'bugs' on view. Right beside the path an ithomiine   butterfly (Ceratinia neso) is hanging beneath a leaf, delicately   dip-

Top: An *Ancyluris* kite-metalmark (Riodinidae) feeding on damp ground.

Above: One of the darker-winged crackers, *Hamadryas amethusa* feeding on mud.

467

Above: *Crocozona coecias* butterfly puddling, a member of the Riodinidae family.

Left: *Callicore hystaspes* feeding on damp ground, one of several nymphalids with a 'numerical' marking on the undersides.

Below: *Darna colorata* (Arctiidae) is one of several warningly coloured day-flying moths that puddle alongside the butterflies.

Below: *Urania leilus* (Uraniidae) is a large day-flying moth that resembles a swallowtail butterfly.

Right: This *Heilipus* weevil is a good example of countershading

Below Right: This *Pteroplatus* longhorn is an excellent lycid beetle mimic.

ping her abdomen onto its surface and depositing her eggs, one at a time. As we walk past a large tree a foul smell assaults our. We search the area for its source, and finally realise that we have been looking straight at the culprits without seeing them. The broad pale trunk of the giant tree is covered with hundreds of incredibly well-camouflaged and very flattened stink-bugs, *Coriplatus depressus*, which are certainly living up to their name, deluging the whole area roundabout with an intense chemical miasma.

We amble onwards—you don't walk quickly when looking for 'bugs', and come into an area that seems to be beetle-city—they are everywhere. The lurid leaf beetle (*Doryphora testudo*) can hardly be missed, as it wears a brilliant warning uniform of black, yellow and red, and there are dozens of them sitting around and converting some unfortunate leaves into tatters. Spotting a *Heilipus* weevil requires a more experienced eye, as its markings includes both countershading and disruptive elements. With its pale upperside and dark underside it looks like a fallen leaf. A pair of *Haplocopturus* weevils mating on a leaf are so tiny they could easily be missed, impressing on us that not all tropical 'bugs' are giants, although plenty certainly are. A *Pteroplatus* longhorn beetle on a nearby plant makes no attempt to conceal itself. It is part of a huge mimicry ring based upon highly distasteful net-winged beetles (Lycidae), and only an experienced field-naturalist would know the difference—a bird would have no chance, which is the whole idea.

Our constantly questing eyes spot some black ants running around on a bush, and we discover that they are tending some large

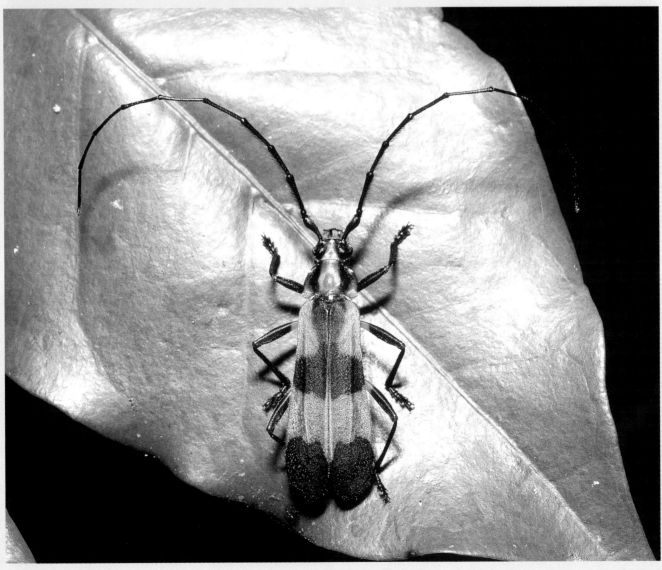

471

groups of *Umbonia spinosa* treehoppers. These are often called thornbugs, because of their supposed mimicry of thorns. In fact, they are far too large to be thorns, and seldom if ever live on thorny trees. They actually employ a triple defence. At a distance their green colouration makes them well camouflaged among leaves. At close range a bright red stripe acts as a warning pattern. If a predator still decides to take a bite, the large spike on the pronotum makes swallowing difficult. This delaying device allows the chemical defences time to come into play, and the bug is spat out. It is a tough insect and unlikely to be damaged by its experience. The females guard their eggs and young nymphs, and will fiercely drive off an enemy with much buzzing and flicking of their wings.

We enter a more open area occupied by a group of well-spaced trees, their trunks mottled with a grey and green growth of lichens and mosses. Some exciting 'bugs' live on bark so it is always worth having a close look, preferably when nobody else is watching—walking round and round dozens of tree trunks, peering intently at the bark could get you some funny looks! We strike lucky on the fourth trunk which harbours a trio of *Acanthodis aquilina* katydids.

These spend their lives sitting head-downwards on tree trunks, where their mottled colours blend perfectly into the bark. If touched they will try and stick their heavily-spined legs in an aggressor's face, and the adult will flash its bright red wings in a distraction display. Tree number seven yields a *Liturgusa* mantis creeping stealthily over the moss-flecked bark. It freezes when it sees us, and instantly blends imperceptibly into its background. Asian and African forests also have similarly cryptic bark-living katydids and mantids, very like these South American examples.

Above the mantis several large *Lystra lanata* lantern fly bugs are sitting in prominent view on the bark. Each has a bunch of slender white waxy 'tails' protruding from its rear end. These are thought to be distasteful to predators and wax is used as a defence by many kinds of bugs around the world. Some lacewing larvae actually harvest the waxy coating from their mealy bug (Coccidae) prey and use it to construct a protective waxy shield over their own backs.

The broad buttress at the base of a giant tree yields us a single specimen of another lantern fly, *Phrictus diadema*. Like most members of its family it has a weird outgrowth on its head—in this

Above: So-called thorn bugs, *Umbonia spinosa* are not really thorn-mimics.

Right: *Liturgusa* mantis on bark.

instance a multi-pronged horn, whose function, as always, is a mystery. This species seems to favour the shaded areas around the buttresses, and the nymphs are strange-looking creatures that resemble large weevils. They suck the sap from the tree trunk, piercing it with a sharp and powerful rostrum.

Continuing along the path, we easily spot a female cocoa stink bug (*Antiteuchus melanoleucus*) standing guard over a large crowd of babies. She is lucky so many have hatched, as the scent from her body actually guides parasitic wasps to her eggs as she stands over them. She can adequately guard most of the eggs, but those at the back often succumb to the persistent intrusions of the wasps. Some very different bugs are on a nearby leaf, greenish-yellow creatures with a thorny outgrowth projecting forwards on either side of the head. This is *Euagona diana* (Coreidae) and it is possibly unique among bugs in being the only known example where the nymphs mimic the adults, in that the top of the nymph's abdomen bears a

pattern that precisely copies the adult's wing arrangement. Just why this should be so is a mystery, but what is certain is that this is one of the most foul-smelling of all bugs, and its thorny outgrowths probably serve the same purpose as a thornbug's thorn, namely making swallowing difficult.

As we straighten up from examining (and smelling) these curious bugs, we realise that another larger bug has been sitting close by all the time. At our sudden movement it raises one of its back legs and starts waving it in the air. The tibia of this leg is greatly enlarged and brilliantly coloured with red and orange blotches, like a flag, hence the name of flag-legged bug for this species (*Anisoscelis foliacea*) and its relatives. This strange leg-waving is primarily intended to make a splash and highlight the warning colours represented by the 'flags' on the legs (these bugs feed on passion flowers and are chemically protected). However, if a bird ignores the message and still takes an experimental bite, it will most likely go for that enticing leg, which the bug can easily afford to leave behind in the enemy's mouth as it makes good its escape. That such a scenario happens fairly often is evident from the number of bugs with one or both back legs missing.

These bugs were in a sunny area, but now we walk into a shadier zone beneath a cliff, crowded with broad-leaf aroids and other shade-loving plants. A 'twig' suddenly begins to walk hesitantly on long spindly legs, giving away the presence of a male *Apioscelis bulbosa* stick grasshopper, which would probably have remained incognito if it had stayed put. It runs rather unsteadily to the edge of the leaf and dives to the ground, where it is immediately a hundred times more difficult to make out among the chaotic mess of

Left: *Lystra lanata*, one of several lantern flies with waxy tails.

Above Right: Cocoa shield bug with babies.

Centre Right: Why should the pattern on the back of this *Euagona diana* nymph resemble the adult's wing-cases?

Right: Adult *Euagona diana*.

leaves and twigs. In fact we have lost it completely and a stick grasshopper's normal escape strategy has proved itself once again.

Looking up, we see an example of the other extreme. A large green and yellow warningly coloured *Chromacris mites* grasshopper is sitting unconcernedly eating a purple flower. On some of the lower leaves is a group of black and red nymphs, using a different warning pattern from the adult, although the latter does have bright red wings that can be exposed to reinforce the message. They are feeding on a bush of the potato family, most of which have poisonous leaves much favoured by these grasshoppers. Despite their overall chemical immunity, they are still vulnerable to attack by unfussy feeders, such as assassin bugs, which seem quite happy to feed on prey that is both foul-tasting and poisonous. Another 'bug' would not even notice its prey's warning colours anyway—these are directed purely at visually-hunting, flavour-sensitive vertebrate predators with good colour vision, such as birds.

We have come back to our starting point after a short circular walk that has shown us some of the world's most fascinating 'bugs'. It is not always like this though, and some rainforest walks will yield little more than irritatingly persistent mosquitoes—it just depends on where you are and when.

Above: *Chromacris* mites grasshopper eating a flower.

Left: Flag-legged bug (*Anisoscelis foliacea*) waving a leg.

Right: Male *Apioscelis bulbosa* stick grasshopper.

6 BUGS AND HUMANS

It is virtually impossible for us to go through life without coming into

contact, at one time or another, with many different kinds of 'bugs'. Taken at the simplest level they may be divided into those that are our 'friends', those that are our 'enemies' and the vast majority, which are neither one nor the other. There will also be times when one person's friend is another's enemy. A hive bee, for example, is great when making honey but not so much fun if it stings you. Let us then look at some of the relationships between ourselves and the hundreds of thousands of 'bugs' that exist in our world.

Insects as Food

To the average person reading this book a plate of scampi or a crab sandwich will probably be very acceptable. Both the prawns in the scampi and the crab are, in effect, sea-dwelling 'bugs'. Offer one of us a plate of roasted grasshoppers, however, and most of us are likely to feel rather sick. Yet, to people in some parts of the world insects are an important and even succulent addition to the diet.

Left: Nsenene katydids (*Ruspolia differens*) having their legs and wings removed before they are fried in oil. Uganda.

Right: Ladybird or ladybug beetles are important predators of injurious aphids, these are *Coccinella transverstoguttata*. USA.

Often shown in natural history documentaries is the 'witchetty grub', the large larva of a cossid moth, which is greatly relished by the Australian aborigines. In Africa the same is true of the 'mopani worm', another moth caterpillar. Whereas the witchetty is usually eaten whole and raw the mopani has to have its gut removed first and it is then baked In a good year hundreds of tons of mopani worms may be eaten. Palm weevil larvae are also considered good eating but they have a negative side as well, for they are pests in commercial palm plantations. A favourite insect food in East Africa is the katydid *Ruspolia differens*, whose local name is nsenene. The wings and legs have to be removed before they are cooked.

With the world population still increasing and more and more of the land being taken up for food production is there a future for 'bugs' as a more widespread source of human food? Insects may not be quite as rich in certain amino acids as, for example, beef but they can be produced much more efficiently. It has been calculated that, in North America, a single hectare of land can, on average, support 100 kilograms (220 pounds) of beef cattle. The same area can, however, support 1,000 kilograms (one ton) of 'bugs'. Whether we will one day see 'bug' farms producing our food is yet to be seen. It will obviously take a lot of education for all of us to accept 'bugs' as food.

Above: A plate of succulent nsenene katydids, crisp fried and ready to eat. Uganda.

Right: Pollination of the blackberry flowers by this *Megachile willughbiella* leaf-cutting bee will result in the juicy fruits which appear in autumn. England.

Below: A plate of giant water bugs and bamboo 'worms' on sale as food on a market stall in Thailand.

Bottom: Giant water bugs in batter on sale in Thailand.

Above: Spiders help control the numbers of insect pests and these money spider webs in a field in autumn show just how numerous they can be. England.

Left: A rhino beetle fighting contest in the sugar cane fields of Thailand.

Right: The comb in which honey bees store their honey and raise their young.

Useful Bugs

Perhaps the one creature that comes to mind for most of us under this heading is the humble hive bee. For centuries this insect has provided us with a source of sweetness and wax, while today, the 'royal jelly' they produce is held in high esteem in homeopathic medicine. This is not, however, their only role since they and many other bees are the main pollinators of many of our fruit and vegetable crops. Ladybird or ladybug beetles are also to be encouraged for they and their larvae are voracious feeders on aphids, many of which are pests on cultivated plants. Web-building spiders prey on many injurious insects, though of course they also take some of our insect friends as well. Other insects that we directly make use of include the silk moth and two species of scale insects. These are plant bugs, most of which are considered as pests but one produces shellac and the other the dye cochineal, though both of these are today being superceded by artificial products.

One relatively new use being made of some insects is in the control of other 'bugs', what we term 'Biological Control'. Under normal conditions in the wild 'bug' numbers are controlled by vertebrates, such as birds, but mainly by other 'bugs', especially spiders and predatory insects. Where these natural predators are unable to control pest numbers we can introduce specially bred examples into a particular habitat to help out. Mealy bugs, one of the plant bugs, are often a pest on glasshouse crops and flowers. It is now possible to buy cultures of a tiny parasitic wasp or a ladybird beetle that can be let loose in a glasshouse infested with the mealybug. The beetle and its larvae then feed directly on the mealybugs while the wasps parasitise them, very quickly bringing the numbers of this pest down, although never eliminating them completely.

In a slightly different context the introduction of some beetles saved sheep and cattle farming in Australia, as follows. Under normal circumstances the dung from our herd animals is broken down fairly rapidly by native insects, most often flies and beetles, whose larvae use it as a source of food. It was soon realised in Australia that pastures were increasingly becoming contaminated by dung, because there were not natural insects to break it down. The answer was to introduce African dung-rolling beetles which soon brought the problem under control and do so to this day.

ATTRACTING BUGS INTO THE GARDEN

One of the great joys of life to many of us is a garden full of colourful flowers that, in turn, are visited by a host of butterflies, bees and other attractive insects, such as hover flies. These days we often plant particular species just to attract these insects. Perhaps the most common of these are the various species of buddleia, which are especially attractive to long-tongued insects such as butterflies, day-flying moths and bumble bees. If, however, you want to attract smaller bees and hover flies, as well as more butterflies, then members of the daisy family, such as dahlias, zinnias and marigolds should be grown.

Right: In the gloom of an approaching storm a snowberry clearwing hawk moth (*Hemaris diffinis*), continues to feed from a buddleia flower. USA.

Below: Hover flies such as *Eristalis transversa* are attractively marked and are keen visitors to garden flowers. USA.

Above: An American bumble bee (*Bombus pennsylvanicus*) forages on a garden zinnia flower. USA.

Above Right: A red admiral butterfly (*Vanessa atalanta*) feeding at a garden sedum flower. England.

Right: A painted lady butterfly (*Vanessa cardui*) feeding on buddleia. England.

Bugs That Bite

One of the worst aspects of 'bugs' is that a number of them bite, not only humans but also domestic animals, and a number are also responsible for passing on some particularly nasty diseases. The biggest culprits are the flies, which include bloodsuckers in several different families. Almost all female mosquitoes feed on blood, at the same time transmitting diseases such as malaria and yellow fever. Less involved in passing on disease but capable of giving a very painful bite are the tabanid flies, which include the horse flies and the deer flies. Tsetse flies do both, acting as carriers of sleeping sickness in humans, domestic animals and wild game and also delivering a painful bite.

The other group which includes members that bite is the true bugs. The bed bug is perhaps the best known of these, though with increased hygiene in the developed world it is less of a problem than it was. Interestingly, the closely related flower bugs, which normally feed on small insects, will, if given the chance, have a go at biting us. The bite can be quite painful and often swells up into a red lump. These bites are probably accidental, although who is to say that they are not on their way to becoming blood feeders. Perhaps less well-known than the bed bugs are the kissing bugs from the southern United States downwards into South America. These are capable of passing on a protozoan infection, Chaga's disease, which can eventually lead to weakening of the heart and death.

Right: Deer flies, this is *Chrysops fulvaster*, have a lighter build than horse flies and have prettily marked wings, though they still deliver a painful bite. USA.

Below Right: This bed bug (*Cimex lectularius*) has emerged at night to take blood from a human finger.

Below: Although it is the females that bite, this male black horse fly (*Tabanus atratus*) still has the rather sinister look of the group as a whole. USA.

Those Pestilential Bugs

Aside from the biters there are many 'bugs' that we consider pests because they impinge in some way or another upon our way of life. It is amongst the insects that we find most of these pests. Perhaps the most obvious cause of nuisance is that they eat or damage our food crops and forests and, maybe less importantly, our beloved garden flowers. Everyone has heard how locusts devastate crops in Africa but swarms of other species of grasshopper behave similarly in other parts of the world. One group of plant bugs, the aphids, cause problems in two ways. They feed directly on the crops by taking sap from them, thus weakening the plants, and they also carry virus infections from plant to plant resulting in further damage. Our planted woodlands also come under attack, especially from various species of moth whose caterpillars strip the leaves from the trees, sometimes leaving large expanses completely leafless and stunting the trees' growth as a result. It should be borne in mind, however, that these insects are really only taking advantage of the fact that we produce enormous areas of a monoculture, which just happens to be their favourite food plant.

Above: A mating pair of one the scourges of the human race, the migratory locust (*Locusta migratoria*).

Right: Someone's beautiful rose being ruined by an attack of rose aphid. England.

Below: A number of cockroach species are worldwide pests, these are Australian cockroaches (*Periplaneta australasiae*) eating a cake in a house at night. Costa Rica.

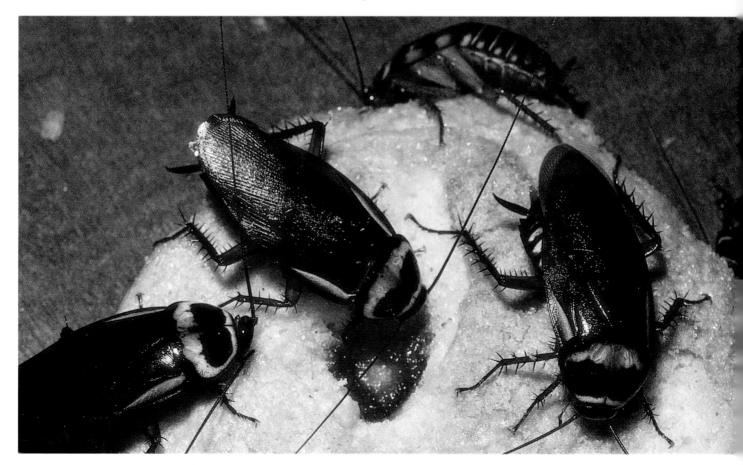

Having harvested our crops or slaughtered our stock, the 'bugs' have still not finished with us. There are numerous species of beetles and moths that feed on stored grain or grain products or even on stored meat. Along with the termites they also attack timber in our buildings and they come into our homes and feed on our clothes, carpets and soft furnishings. Cockroaches are a great nuisance in many parts of the world, feeding on and spoiling any food that is left uncovered.

Top: A Colorado beetle (*Leptinotarsa decimlineata*) which can be a serious pest on potato crops.

Above: Box elder bugs (*Leptocoris trivittatus*) can cause premature leaf-fall in forests in years when they occur in huge numbers. USA.

Right: Cottonstainer bugs, *Dysdercus sp.*, feeding on cassava, an important human food in Africa. Kenya.

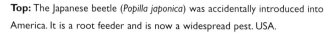

Top: The Japanese beetle (*Popilla japonica*) was accidentally introduced into America. It is a root feeder and is now a widespread pest. USA.

Above: In our homes larvae of the carpet beetle (*Anthrenus verbasci*) damage carpets and other woolen goods. England.

Top: The spotted cucumber beetle (*Diabrotica undecimpunctata*) is a pest of members of the pumpkin family. USA.

Above: The face of that important transmitter of a number of human diseases—the house fly (*Musca domestica*). England.

Right: Caterpillars of the buff-tip moth (*Phalera bucephala*) feed on the leaves of a number of trees and can be pests. England.

Overleaf: Case-bearing clothes moths (*Tinea pellionella*) on a woollen jumper which they have damaged. England.

ARACHNOPHOBIA

No, not a review of the well-known film of this title but a few words about a very common human affliction. From personal experience it would seem that a large proportion of people—male and female—have an irrational fear of spiders. Irrational because there are no spiders anywhere that approach us in size and very few spiders are capable of harming us in any way whatsoever. The most common explanation for the phobia is that they are hairy and that they scuttle, but then kittens and puppies are hairy and crabs scuttle yet most folks are quite happy to handle them. So maybe there is no real answer to our phobia.

An interesting development in recent years, however, seems to point to the fact that some of us at least are coming to terms with our arachnophobia. Increasingly, people are keeping spiders as pets, and not little spiders but those big, hairy 'tarantulas'. Despite their size and the fact that they are big enough to deliver a painful bite they seldom do so and those that are kept as pets produce a poison that is no worse than a wasp sting. Some of the spiders kept as pets are very attractive and collecting them from the wild has posed a threat to some. Luckily, most of them can now be bred quite successfully and the pressures on wild populations have thus been reduced.

Above: The face view of that loathed but harmless member of many households, the house spider (*Tegenaria sp.*). England.

Above Right: The grand salmon-pink spider (*Lasiodora parahybana*) one of the tarantulas bred for collectors.

Below Right: The emperor scorpion (*Pandinus imperator*) which is keenly sought by collectors.

Below: A captive-bred red-kneed tarantula (*Brachypelma smithi*) a species very popular with collectors.

Poisonous Bugs

There are no 'bugs' that purposefully poison us, for we are far too big to be prey, and all human poisonings are accidental or a result of the animal defending itself against what it perceives to be a threat. The most obvious of this group of creatures are the poisonous arachnids—the spiders and the scorpions. Best documented are the 'widow spiders', the notorious black widows and their close relatives. A number of species of black widow are known, from the Americas, Europe and Australia. The southern black widow of the USA can be very common, the underside of virtually every air-conditioning unit and the stairwells of most motels having a number of these spiders present in their webs. It is no wonder that we accidentally come into contact with them when, if pressured in some way, they bite in self-defense. Luckily, for their venom is ten times as toxic as rattlesnake venom, widows are small spiders and they deliver a tiny dose. The poison attacks the nervous system resulting in breathing difficulties and muscle cramps but only rarely, usually in tiny children or adults with weak hearts, is it ever fatal. Fatalities are, however, more likely to occur with bites from the funnel web spiders of Australia and the *Phoneutria sp.* wandering spiders from South America, for both are larger than the widows and deliver more venom. Again, it is young children who are most likely to die from the bite, especially that of the wandering spider. One reason for this is that whereas in Australia antitoxins to neutralize the affects of the bite are available, this is seldom the case in the less developed countries of South America.

Another family, sometimes simply called the brown spiders, contains a number of species whose poison acts in a different way. Like the widows they are small and bites occur by accident. The poison causes local tissue death and if left untreated this can spread over a larger area resulting in huge ulcers that can take months to heal.

Despite their being larger than most of the poisonous spiders the scorpions only cause occasional deaths, especially in Central America, though their stings can be excruciatingly painful. Interestingly, there is no relationship between the size of the sting and how poisonous they are, the worst stings being found among the smaller species. Much more dangerous are the giant centipedes of Asia, which can reach up to 30 centimetres (ten inches) in length. They can deliver a bite that is extremely painful and although seldom fatal to adults has been known to kill small children.

A

Left: The walkingstick *Anisomorpha buprestoides* squirts an irritant fluid into the eyes of its enemies when attacked. USA.

Right: Velvet ants, in fact a kind of wasp, have a very painful sting; this is the 'cow-killer' (*Dasymutilla occidentalis*). USA.

Studying Bugs

The study of 'bugs' has long held a fascination for a small proportion of the human race and today there are still many professional entomologists and arachnologists. Amongst these are the taxonomists, whose sole concern is the collection, identification and naming of insects and spiders, the behaviourists, who study 'bug' life-styles and the ecologists and conservationists, who are interested in their distribution and conservation.

Not all of us can aspire to being professional entomologists or arachnologists but at least it is possible to be a competent amateur. There are plenty of field guides available, both in the United Kingdom and in North America, to help us to recognise the most common insects and spiders. In addition, there are groups, such as the Bees, Wasps and Ants Recording Society in the United Kingdom, who welcome amateur as well as professional entomologists. Many of these groups now have internet websites and using key words such as 'beetle' or 'spider' in a search engine will help you to find details about them.

Although it is possible to identify many common 'bugs' in the field, this is not the case for the majority of species and in order to find out precisely what species they are they will have to be collected. One important thing to remember when you are collecting, however, is that some species have been sent close to extinction by over-greedy enthusiasts and you should only take one specimen of a particular species. It is always best to take a male, if you can recognise it as such. Collecting can be done in many ways, depending on what you are interested in. Free-flying insects can be taken in a butterfly net, insects and spiders on bushes and low vegetation can be taken in a more robust sweep net. Alternatively a white sheet can be laid out on the ground and the 'bugs' can be beaten off the vegetation above it using a stick. Insects and spiders amongst leaf litter may then be sorted out on the white sheet or tray. Finally, for ground-dwelling insects it is possible to set up pitfall traps, jars sunk into the ground with their tops level with the surface. It is usual to put a cover over them to stop rain entering, obviously the cover should be raised a little so the 'bugs' can fall in, and they should have a couple of centimeters depth of 70 per cent alcohol in the bottom to kill and preserve the 'bugs' that fall in. Visit them regularly!

Left: Native peoples walking barefoot through the rainforest have to watch their step.

Below: A selection of collected butterflies from Southeast Asia.

It is not necessary to kill all of the 'bugs' that you have collect-ed, for some of them will be identifiable while they are still alive. If this is the case then please return them to where you found them if this is at all possible. Otherwise you will have to kill them and this is best done using ethyl acetate soaked cotton wool in a jar. It is much safer to use than cyanide and relaxes the 'bugs' so that they maintain their colours, but one thing to remember is that it is imflammable. Tough insects such as beetles can be placed in tubes for transporting them back home but delicate winged insects, such as butteflies and moths, will need to be placed carefully into folds of paper to transport them. Once you have got them home they can be pinned and placed on cork or expanded polystyrene sheets to help keep them intact. For identification, as well as a key or field guide, you will find a binocular microscope very useful.

Right: A mosaic of rainforest and farmland in Rondonia. Brazil.

Below: The common swallowtail (*Papilio machaon*) a species which has thrived as a result of active conservation of its habitat. England.

Bug Conservation

Since 'bugs' are found in just about every habitat on the surface of the earth then conservation of any habitat will preserve all of the species that live in it. Concerned people everywhere are doing their best to ensure that something at least of every important habitat on earth is protected but this is not always possible. It is an understandable fact of life that a family on the brink of starvation are not going to think twice about slashing and burning pristine rainforest to grow crops if it will ensure their survival. Who are we to condemn when in the United Kingdom, for example, sites of special scientific interest are regularly ploughed up, built on, converted to carparks or flooded to form marinas, destroying the 'bugs' and other wildlife that live there, all in the name of money and progress. At least some countries are getting their act togeth-er, despite enormous pressures from burgeoning populations. In the Rondonia area of the Amazonian rainforest in Brazil, for example, farmers are permitted to cut down only 50 per cent of the forest. The rest remaining as an important conservation area, which contains more species of butterflies, for example, than any other place on earth.

The only way to ensure that we can conserve at least something of everything is to have a global understanding of how important

'bugs' and their role in the balance of nature are to all of us. Sadly, it is certain that this understanding will be a long time in coming and in the intervening period we will lose forever many species of 'bug' that we never even knew existed.

Left: Male *Heliconius erato* butterflies in their communal roost at night in the Rondonia conservation area. Brazil.

Below: The large copper butterfly (*Lycaena dispar*) now sadly extinct in the British Isles, partly as a result of habitat destruction.

Glossary of Biological Terms

Abdomen—the rear part of the 'bug' body containing internal organs such as the heart, the main digestive system and the reproductive organs.

Antennae—structures on the head sensitive to air movement, touch or airborne chemical scents.

Batesian mimicry—where a palatable 'bug' (the mimic) resembles an unpalatable or poisonous 'bug' (the model). The mimic, therefore, falsely gains the same level of protection from visually hunting enemies such as birds, as the model.

Caudal appendages—feelers on the end of the abdomen found in cockroaches and other insects and developed as pincers in the earwig.

Cephalothorax—the name given to the single structure formed by the fusing together of the head and thorax regions of the body in spiders.

Cerci—see caudal appendages.

Chelicerae—the hinged jaws of spiders and other arachnids.

Compound eyes—the main eyes of insects which, in effect, are made up of hundreds or even thousands of tiny individual eyes, each with its own lens.

Ecdysis—the shedding of the old body covering in 'bugs' to permit growth.

Elytra—the forewings of beetles which are modified to form hard, protective cases for the delicate, flying hindwings.

Fangs—the piercing section of arachnid jaws or the specially modified poisonous appendages of a centipede.

Flagellum—the long tail-like structure on the end of the abdomen of a whip-scorpion.

Halteres—club-shaped structures, which have replaced the hind-wings in flies and are concerned with balance during flight.

Instars—the name given to the stages between each moult during 'bug' development after hatching from the egg.

Jaws—structures used by bugs for biting and chewing.

Larva—developmental stage of an insect, in butterflies and moths usually referred to as a caterpillar.

Mandibles—the tough, biting segments of a 'bug's' jaws.

Maxillae—the more delicate slicing and cutting segments of a 'bug's' jaws which lie behind the mandibles and are not normally visible.

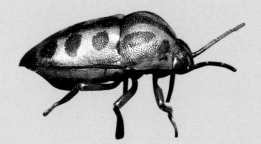

Moult—shedding of the old body covering.

Müllerian mimicry—where two or more species of unpalatable or poisonous 'bugs' exhibit a similar warning pattern. By wearing the same 'uniform' all the members of a mimicry ring gain because their enemies only have to memorise a single pattern. Most mimicry rings include both Müllerian and Batesian mimics.

Nymph—an alternative name for an instar in some insects.

Obelisk position—a stance adopted by dragonflies: by pointing their abdomen directly at the sun they avoid taking in too much heat energy.

Ocelli—simple eyes, which detect the difference between light and dark rather than forming complex images.

Ocularium—a protuberance of the head of a harvestman on which the eyes are situated.

Ovipositor—tube through which the female 'bug' lays her eggs.

Pedipalps or palps—appendages on the front of the face, associated with the jaws and involved in tasting food for its edibility.

Pheromones—chemical sex attractants which are often, though not always, transported between the sexes in air currents.

Proboscis—a tubular modification of the jaws used for taking up liquid food.

Pupa—a resting stage in some insects during which the larval form is converted into the adult.

Rostrum—another name for the proboscis or, in weevils, the forward, tubular extension of the face at the end of which are the jaws.

Spermatophore—a package of sperm produced by some male 'bugs'.

Sphragis—a plug in the reproductive opening of an already mated female preventing other males from mating with her.

Stabilimentum—an area of special ultraviolet reflecting silk built into the webs of some spiders.

Stridulation—production of sound by usually a male 'bug' to attract a mate.

Thorax—the section of an insect body on which arise the legs and wings.

Index